I0030528

No Nonsense Inside Sales

Your Complete Guide to Mastering the Art of Inside Selling in the 21st Century

Paul   Archer

HH

High House Publishing

Copyright © Paul Archer 2022

This book is copyrighted under the Berne Convention.

No reproduction without permission.

All rights reserved. The right of Paul Archer to be identified as the author of this work has been asserted by him in accordance with sections 77 and 78 of the Copyright Designs and Patents Act, 1988. All rights reserved.

No part of this publication may be reproduced, stored in a retrieval system, or transmitted in any form, or by any means, electronic, mechanical, photocopying, recording, and/or otherwise without the proper permission of the publishers.

This book may not be lent, resold, hired out, or otherwise disposed of by way of trade in any form, binding, or cover other than that in which it is published, without the prior consent of the publishers.

First published in Great Britain in 2016 by High House Publishing, Tivoli Studios, Cheltenham, Gloucestershire, GL50 2UG, United Kingdom.

Printed and bound in Great Britain by Lulu.com.

Second Edition.

Copy edited by Angie Bruce

Cover designed by Shelley White

ISBN 978-0-9933112-4-6 (Paperback)

ISBN 978-0-9933112-5-3 (eBook)

For all your sales coaching needs, in-house requirements, contact Paul at:

paul@paularcher.com
www.paularcher.com

+44 (0)7702 341769

This book is dedicated to my father Denis Archer, a sales rep all his life who inspired me to enter the field of sales and 35 years later, here I am. He lives happily in rural France. Thanks Pops.

Table of Contents

Introduction

In the chapter later in this book – 15 Predictions for Sales – I talk about how Inside Sales is changing rapidly and will continue to do so. Metamorphosing of Inside Sales. Yes we have the advance of technology of course, with increasingly sophisticated ways to communicate with customers – video, virtual reality, augmented reality – these will revolutionise the way we sell from inside, naturally. But that's not the transformation I foresee.

Let me explain.

Back in the day, sales led companies operated one or more of three business models according to the sophistication of their products and customers.

For the high end long complex sales, we had account managers who would farm a collection of accounts often called key accounts. They were consultants by nature, helping the customer to achieve their aims and to use the product they sold. The good ones were very highly skilled at ensuing they were up to speed with the customer's issues, problems and challenges and offered expert guidance and advice around their product area. The best ones had a reputation as thought leaders in their field and were highly respected in their customer's eyes.

For commodity type sales which required a boot on the ground, we had sales representatives – or reps. These salespeople would call on a set of customers, big and small. They would be the voice of the company and knew everything about their products. The good ones would also be consultative but they were heavily targeted to achieve sales of their product range. Their cars had large boots to store all the samples they carried around.

Finally for order taking selling and low end commodity sales, we had the call centre taking inbound calls and collecting orders from customers. The good ones were also proactive in nature and made outbound calls to sell the product or to fix appointments for the account managers or sales reps to enjoy.

Then along came the internet and the buyer adopting a more "in control" attitude. No longer did they need brochures or samples, since these could be effortlessly obtained from the internet. Modern buyers – consumers and businesses alike – enjoyed this new control so they extended it and now complete large swathes of the old sales process that we used to operate. They like being in control and no longer see the need for a brochure pitching salesperson because they can choose the products themselves.

So how is the model evolving? Simply put…the middle one has been squeezed and the two outer layers have taken up the slack.

The old rep has gone or will go. Account managers continue so long as they consult and advise but the greatest opportunity is for the Inside Salesperson. And the best ones will simply operate the same sales process as the account managers and conduct this indoors, using the various technological innovations that allow us to communicate to customers. There's no difference apart from not being face to face. But with ubiquitous super-fast fibre and broadband and the introduction of virtual reality systems, in the future we may not even notice the difference.

This book is dedicated to the Inside Salesperson of the future. She stays indoors but for all intents and purposes assumes the role of the account manager. She has a selection of accounts that she calls upon, influences many people within the accounts, knows her industry sector well and the challenges facing it.

She has internal networks of people who can help her achieve her targets. She's incredibly dextrous with technology and can pick up new systems and programmes effortlessly. She's a great communicator, motivator and can motivate herself from inside – internally motivated. In short she's the future of sales.

The New Bazaar for Inside Sales Teams

Why do we have Inbound Selling?

You've heard the term – Inbound Sales or Inbound Marketing – and you may feel it's a fad that will come and go. It really isn't.

At my gym we have a team of personal trainers whose job is to support our fitness goals. They come alongside you, see where you are and what you want to achieve and then support you along the way with insightful advice and ideas to make the most of your journey. They do not push too much; sell you health supplements or a new contract. They're there to support you.

In the same way, this is how inbound selling works or should work.

We are faced with:

- Buyers are in control and use the internet to research solutions and obtain references from their networks. They want to do the buying themselves.
- Buyers don't need salespeople anymore, not traditional ones.

They have their buying process. As an inbound salesperson we need to be adept at knowing what this is and when the customer makes contact, we need to quickly ascertain where they are on their journey and then support them, just like my personal trainer.

It's not that much more complex.

A new sales process

We create and align our sales process alongside theirs with the sole aim of supporting their buying so they keep control. Beforehand we need to study carefully who our buyers are, what problems and struggles they have, what solutions they are researching, where we can help.

We provide content, a lot of content. We work alongside marketing to create and disperse this. The content we put out is all about answers, expertise, solutions that we know full well the clients are seeking. We put out blog posts, articles on various websites, white papers which bring the customer to our website. Videos on YouTube and Vimeo, our social media streams are full of solutions and links to content. We constantly update this content with new ideas and solutions and we make them accessible to all prospective buyers. When they're ready they'll find their way to our website.

A client case study

One area of specialism I have is selling protection products for financial advisers. I smother the web with my articles and writings, videos and podcasts which teach salespeople how to perform this vital skill. Just last week I received an email from a prospective corporate client who runs a chain of mortgage brokers on the south coast. His email stated that he'd been researching and found my writings, in fact it was mainly LinkedIn that allowed him to find me. We began talking on the phone this week and my first objective was to align my sales process with where he was with his research.

He told me once I asked the question: "How far are you in your search for a solution here?"

He mentioned that he'd researched the web for ideas and articles and found mine. He'd passed the thought process about doing it himself, as he's really busy. He was at the final selection of provider stage and was concerned about removing or illuminating any risk in his decision. So that's where I started – remove risk, fact-find and proposal stage.

It all sounds rather soothing, never having to cold call or push a customer along the sales process but in reality it will be different for you. As a full time inside salesperson, you'll have targets to achieve and a manager on your back if you don't. She'll be measuring against some very traditional sales KPIs and may not be bought into the concept of inbound selling. A few things need to be changed if you're going to succeed in this new bazaar.

The salesperson's role

I've already mentioned the need to put out content alongside your marketing colleagues.

You also need to be very adept at monitoring activity and analytics from your websites and social media streams so you can pick up potential customers who are browsing and downloading whitepapers and other specialist content. Many companies ask for full contact details to download white papers and the like. This is dangerous and you can put off a buyer who wants to maintain their anonymity and control. An email is fine but not address and phone number. Seriously, this will hamper your progress.

So you have a buyer on your website who's just downloaded some content or has started following you on Twitter or Facebook. What do you do? The worst sin is to pick up the phone and try your old sales process or email a request for an appointment. Just don't to this, your role is to support their buying.

You email them and subtly ask if they have any questions to ask about the content they downloaded. Or you offer them some more content that might help them. Recently I noticed a corporate customer link in with me and follow me on Twitter. Instead of emailing them or phoning them to fix up an appointment, I stopped and thought, what's going to be their major concern and struggle at the moment and why are they wanting to link in with me?

They were from a company that advised second mortgages and loans to consumers. Now because I keep my ear to the ground, I knew that they were going to be thinking about regulation under the Financial Services Act which kicked in for these companies in 2016. I knew they were thinking about Training and Competence schemes and exam training for their teams. I emailed my new contact with a White Paper entitled "How to Create a Training and Competence Scheme for Regulated Companies".

This white paper tells them everything I know; the lot. I don't leave anything out to entice them to call. If they want to solve the problem or give the paper to their training manager – that's fine. My value position is not to just deliver training anymore, it's to consult and provide tailored solutions for corporate clients. If she wanted to do it herself that's fine, if not I'm here and she knows it.

I put her details into my CRM and incubator, as I call it. She's now receiving regular updates from me in the form of sales tips and videos and the odd long-form article.

As an inbound salesperson, you need to be able to provide additional support for any buyer. You need to be crystal clear as to your buyer – who she is and the challenges she faces – this is why you fully understand your marketplace. This knowledge makes you very different to traditional salespeople and you are able to consult rather than just sell.

You'll have a CRM system – something like Hubspot – which allows for email campaigns and auto responders to be sent out as soon as someone enters the database. These emails contain useful further information, download links and personalised suggestions.

Say you're into website optimisation as a business and a contact is made. You may email an article on search engine optimisation with Bing, but you've also been onto their site and realise there's a couple of quick fixes that the customer can do themselves, so you put this in the email as friendly advice.

You support them. You know their buying sequence – which normally looks like this:

1. Problem awareness
2. Research
3. Decision

If they're in research mode- help them to do so. When they get into decision mode, help them to do this, but don't be pushy – remember buyers don't need or even like salespeople anymore.

Just like the buyer who has more information than ever at their fingertips, in the same way the salesperson also has enormous amounts of data and information. So use it. Seek out prospective customers, those who may be struggling with a problem that you can solve. Put yourself in their way online. Join in discussion forums where they hang out. Know where they might hang out and be there: forums, discussion groups, webinar audiences, on line conferences.

The sales manager's role

In my experience the manager finds this transition to inbound sales the biggest challenge. Their job is to produce revenue from their team of sellers and they receive intense pressure from above for this to happen. Inbound selling can take longer to get going so if the manager is looking for quick results, they may revert back to the old way.

It's a new philosophy.

The manager is the first person to buy into the concept and then provide support and encouragement to their teams. Their coaching and observations must change to support a different set of skills. They must think about recruitment – what kind of individual is better served in the new bazaar? They consider training – is this fit for purpose?

The sales trainer's role

The old way of sales training doesn't work anymore – prospecting, cold calling, overcoming objections, closing techniques. People still demand it and sales trainers still deliver it.

But in the world of inbound selling a whole new range of skill sets are needed.

I read about a technology company in the USA who ran a very interesting on boarding training scheme for their team's inside salespeople. They were asked to get under the skin of their potential buyer, to understand who they were and mimic their situation as much as possible. This company's customers were small business owners who wanted to drive more traffic through their websites and their main product offering was a CRM system that would make this objective far easier to achieve.

They set up a mock company to mirror their potential buyer.

They found out how their buyers researched, where they researched, what questions did they have unanswered from the research, what information did they seek, where did they get this from. This way our new salespeople knew where to post content and what questions to ask their buyers when contact was made.

Then the salespeople were tasked to dive into their buyer's world even more by setting up their own micro business and creating a website and social media streams to solve the problem of new business generation. This allowed them to realise the problems and produce solutions from their own expertise.

The result. They became accustomed to helping the buyer, supporting them in their quest rather than wanting to sell them their products. They had changed their philosophy. That's effective training.

It's a mind-set change, it won't go away, the old days of cold calling prospects and pushing them along the sales process set by head office are long gone or are leaving your industry for good. Are you ready to change?

If Only I Had More Customers

Practical and tactical strategies to get more customers into your sales funnel for small business owners.

Over the weekend, I received an email from one of my LinkedIn connections.

"I'm an avid follower and reader of your emails ever since you helped me many years ago. I've recently entered the Business Protection market. I've attended several seminars, numerous webinars and studied profusely regarding this subject; and I'm now ready. I now just need to get the contacts and audience. Any tips?"

And here's my reply for anyone else in the same boat.

Target your marketing strategies

As a small business owner you need to be careful with your marketing budget and time since you generally have little of each. The first thing you need to do is to analyse where your business comes from, that's assuming you've been trading up to that point.

I analyse where my business comes from each year and gear my marketing spend and time towards generating the same. The last survey revealed:

- 30% from existing client referrals

- 40% from my network referrals

- 15% from Inbound Marketing and my websites and blogs

- 15% from my weekly sales tip emailing to my database

These produced leads which I put into my sales funnel, which directs to a close.

Remember this point – it's really important. Marketing is fine and effective marketing will produce sales leads. It still requires a salesperson to close the lead into business. Many small business owners forget this but need to have created their sales funnel and their sales process within the funnel.

My friend needs to do this and if he doesn't have any existing business, then he ought to research how someone like him gains new business. Knowing the sector, I suspect it comes from:

- Existing active client referrals at 50%

- Network referrals at 15%

- Buying leads on the internet and other bought data at 25%

- Orphaned clients (old ones where no business has been conducted for a while) at 15%

These are my best guesstimates but also prove the point that it's pointless doing other marketing if it doesn't actually work.

Be wary of internet marketing

Be very wary of internet marketing, social media, search engine optimising your website for leads, paying for online advertising. Every day I get emails from so called SEO companies offering to get my website higher up the rankings. I read a blog post from my friend Graham Jones who reported that it's very easy to get lured into online marketing for two reasons.

One, it's actually quite easy to do, is faceless and you don't get any rejection from prospective customers.

Two, it's dead easy to measure how successful it is but not how much business it produces. It's simple to add up your Twitter followers, how many Facebook followers you have, how many "likes" your latest article received and how many retweets you had. These stats give people pleasure and the illusion that it works.

So back to my financial adviser friend and how he can get some prospective clients.

Your sales process

Once he's analysed how he can put people into his sales funnel, he needs a database management tool to act as his CRM, to create his sales process, wrap it into his CRM and stick to it rigidly. CRMs don't have to be enterprise level and costly. Something like Nimble or Pipeline will do just as well at $10 per month.

My sales process looks like:

- Qualify over the phone or Skype video – Are they a fit for my business and are they motivated, have they the budget and is there a business challenge that needs addressing?

- Face to face meeting or Skype video to determine needs/problems and the solution I can recommend.

- Further meeting to run through proposal (I will not email a proposal to a new prospect and hope and pray they accept it – this is not a good strategy).

- Close the business.

- Conduct the business and seek referrals.

Let's see how we can put some prospective clients into my friend's new pipeline that he can channel into his sales process.

Where to start

Referrals is where I would start.

Sieve through your client bank and see which have a need for business insurance. Are they self-employed or run their own small business? Easy to judge.

Contact them to offer a complimentary review of their financial circumstances. Speak to them on the phone, don't do email or letters, these get deleted unless they're a very close client. Phone them on their mobile, contact them outside of office hours – early in the morning is good. Prepare a voice mail message to guarantee they return your call and have a sound bite ready.

Telephone prospecting pattern

Follow this pattern:

- Introduce yourself.

- Suggest the challenge they may be experiencing i.e. knowing who'll take on their business if something tragic happens and they're no longer around.

- Suggest you have some really tax efficient, low cost and exciting ways of handling this.

- Call to action.

Have two calls to action ready. One would be an immediate face to face appointment to discuss further. Two might be to send them something via email to capture their email address, if you haven't already got one. A White Paper that you've written on the solution to the challenge you mentioned, or a YouTube video link of you describing the problem that small business owners have and the solutions you have available.

Put the appointments into your CRM system and begin your sales process with them. For the others, they need to go into your CRM naturally but activate the incubator with them.

Your incubator

What's this incubator? Just like you would put newly laid eggs into an incubator to ensure they all hatch at some point, you would put those who are not ready to enter your sales process into your own incubator. The incubator keeps them warm and keeps your name in front of them without you appearing like a pest.

My incubator consists of a database mailing system using Mailchimp where I email, every week, a short sales and coaching tip and a link to a brand new video clip. My friend receives this and prompts him to email me.

One on Sunday and the other on Tuesday. The same system emails out links to new White Papers, new videos, other articles, requests to LinkIn with me, special reports.

I would suggest that my friend begins an email system like Mailchimp and starts writing and producing content that demonstrates his expertise in his area of specialism. The purpose of this content is to prove your value, show that you handle the issues every day and are very experienced at it and keep your "name in the frame".

Within my funnel I have a section for prospects who are really "hot" but don't want a meeting yet. This segment of my incubator get special treatment. Cards, White Papers, other articles of interest, phone calls to see what they thought of the article or video etc.

I suggest my friend does the same.

Automate this in your CRM otherwise you'll not have the time to cope with it all and when you get super busy you won't do any of it at all.

This sequence of calling people is the same however you received the lead. Let's talk about how we can get some more leads other than harvesting this existing client bank.

Set up a referral system

Set up a referral system and stick to it. Many small business owners are referred particularly if they do a good job. But many just wait for them. This is fine but if you want more, you need to ask. Have a system.

Mention to all new clients that you grow your business by referrals, that way you can concentrate on giving them a superb personalised service. Do this during your introduction, not later on. The when you've given them a superb service, ask them if they know of anyone in their network who would also value the benefits and value you've given them. Suggest people in their network, other business owners, friends who are self-employed.

I've even used the "If we swapped jobs right now and you did what I do, who would be the first three people you'd call?"

Use LinkedIn

Use the LinkedIn testimonials facility to add to the referral. Ask your client to LinkIn with you and then use their contacts. Have a look at their contacts to see if there are any small business owners on their list, if so, ask politely using LinkedIn's own system to have an introduction.

Use LinkedIn's advanced search capability to look up all small business owners in your locality. LinkedIn will display these people and show you who they are connected to, from your network. That way, you contact your network person and ask them to refer you. Simple and it works too.

Energy and time spent doing this will reap dividends, it's hard work, full of potential rejection which is why trying to gain more website visitors and followers on Twitter appears more interesting but less efficient.

Buying data or leads

There are plenty of places where you can buy a database to trawl or buy individual leads of people who have just indicated online that they would be interested in speaking to someone about their needs.

A good friend of mine runs a similar business to the one we're talking about here and gets 50% of his business from purchased mortgage leads. He hired a part-time telephone person to make calls to these leads to generate an appointment for him. I helped them to refine their calling script with some really effective results. The leads he buys cost him, naturally, but in the great scheme of things, it is just a marketing spend.

The other 50% comes from client referrals which he actively seeks. He has a robust and profitable small business.

With a lead, you still have to call them immediately, otherwise the lead cools down. And you need to have a script and sound bites ready similar to the one we mentioned earlier. However it needs tailoring to reflect what the prospect was doing prior to your call. Again potential rejection, so get used to it. If rejection brings you down, speak to me and I'll advise on ways you can remove this limiting belief.

Websites and advertising

I sincerely wouldn't get involved here. Yes, you need a website of course; I would suggest more of a blog where your content is published. Unless you have a budget equal to a big bank, then online advertising is just going to cost you money. All the keywords my friend needs to promote cost hundreds of pounds a click and the big players operate in this area.

Build your network on LinkedIn

Begin to add contacts of people you know and trust, past clients and all people you meet when you attend business events, seminars, etc. You never know, who you meet might provide you with a referral one day. My friend's trade association requires that he carries out oodles of CPD – continued professional development. I think all of us should. I spend a day a week on my CPD, yes that's a day a week. So when you attend these seminars and courses, meet people, help them and refer each other. But LinkIn with them always.

If you get a request to LinkIn and you will as your contacts grow, arrange a simple telephone conversation to discover their business and challenges for 10 minutes. Use LinkedIn's own email system as people answer these. You'll be amazed at how many people agree to this call.

I do this all the time. People on my database ask to LinkIn with me, website and blog visitors ask. I call them PQCs – prospect qualifying calls – and these allow me to put people into my funnel if I can help them in their business.

Summary

So my LinkedIn friend, here are the ways in which you can find people to talk to tailored specifically to your business. They will work, so spend a day a week on your marketing and don't ever give up on this.

Even when you're stupidly busy, keep marketing. Outsource much of it if you like. Know the difference between marketing and selling – selling is the hardest since there's the prospect of rejection. You don't get rejected with marketing on a personal level, you do when you're selling and closing.

And above all, don't get sucked into the hype of social media, retweeting, followers, blog comments, Google advertising and the like. It's very comforting but won't get you the new business that'll keep you profitable and successful. Pre-emptive Selling

Pre-Emptive Sales Consulting

In this chapter, I'm going to bring you up to speed with the modern business buyer's buying process and how the internet has helped them to treat our products and services as commodities.

The reason? Simple, they're now more than ever in control and bring us in when they're evaluating options to solve their problems and challenges that they have recognised.

Get the picture? They're in control.

The answer is to adopt pre-emptive selling techniques by approaching the business buyer far earlier than we've ever done in their buying process. Before even they have recognised the need or problems.

That way we can influence, become a valuable resource and truly add value to our product or service.

Nuclear holocaust

"Quick…under the table, now". As a child I recall, with fondness, the training to avoid nuclear meltdown, not that hiding under a table would protect you from a 10 kiloton nuclear warhead.

But in those days it was all about trying to get a pre-emptive strike in before the enemy could retaliate, hence the need for immediate hiding under the table. Warfare had changed in a few years and the secret was to attack early before the enemy had time to react.

In the old days of warfare, combatants had plenty of time to mobilise troops, ship them out to theatres of battle and organise their supply columns. Modern warfare in my youth had changed so that speed and an early response were deemed necessary.

The same has happened to selling, both selling to consumers and selling to other businesses. You can't wait anymore until everyone's ready to buy as you'll miss the boat.

You have to get in earlier.

The changing buying process

The reason, as you know, is the changing buying process. Customers are beginning their buying cycle way before they call us in to satisfy their needs. The graph below shows you that salespeople are brought in now at about 57% along the customer's buying process. That's way too late and forces you down the commodity transaction where you're squeezed on price and terms.

Our first foray into sorting this out was consultative selling. Here the seller would attempt to meet with the customer before he brought them in to quote. Here the seller would ask questions about their business, problems and challenges in order to recommend a solution to these needs – the classic consultative sale.

Obstacles and barriers are being thrown at the consultative seller now. Gatekeepers, voice mail, time challenged buyers are not playing the game anymore and if you do manage to get through to a buyer, you need to be fully aware of their issues before you enter their office.

The secret is to enter the fray way before the buyer has even realised they have problems and need to do something to solve them. This is pre-emptive selling and will enable you to enter businesses near the top, provoke a need and begin conversations way before the buyer traditionally brings in vendors.

The modern buyer's buying process

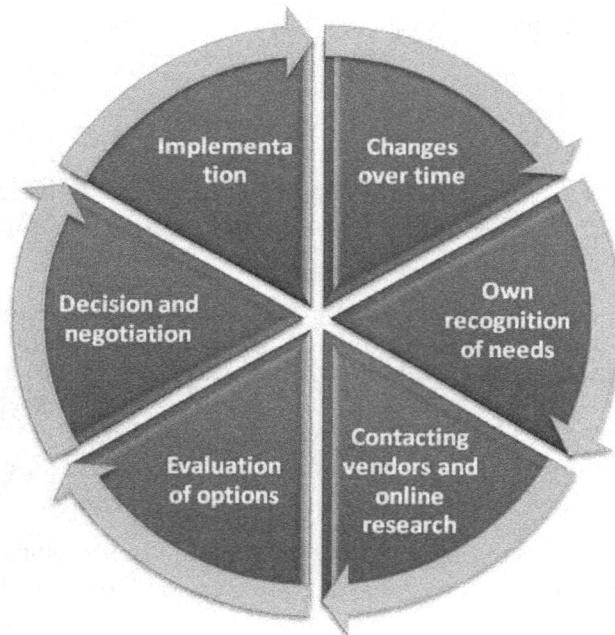

Pre-emptive strike

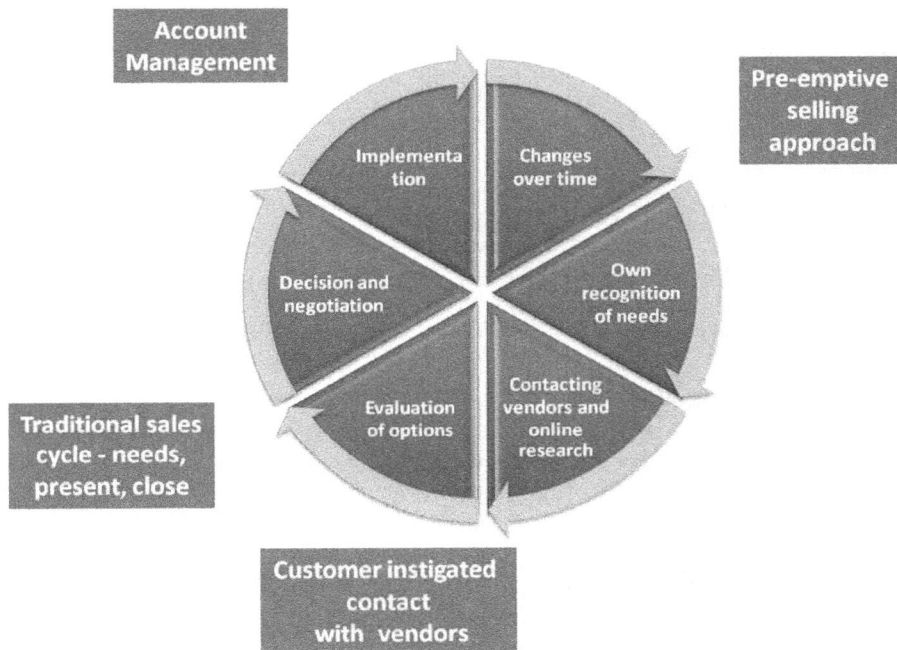

The 6 steps to pre-emptive selling success

Here are the key steps to evolve into pre-emptive selling. Many of these steps will be familiar to you, if not all, but it's the order of their implementation that's vital to success.

1. Know your added value

Know the specific value you provide over and above your product or service. Yes your product or service provides value, of course it does, but if you're bought in by customers when they are looking for a business solution, then they'll attempt to treat your product or service as a commodity. I've been there many times. A customer calls me up out of the blue and wants to talk about my training services. One of the first questions they ask is how much, what's my delivery fee? Naturally they're comparing this with other vendors and are treating the delivery as a commodity.

It's the added value you bring to the table, the service you provide, the personalisation you bring, the something extra. If you don't then you are doomed.

2. Segment your market acutely

So you can become an expert on the challenges facing your customers and the ins and outs of their worlds, you mustn't spread yourself too widely, otherwise this becomes an impossible task. Many are reluctant not wishing to turn away business, but the key fact is, you can't be a jack of all trades and master of none.

Be brave and segment your market carefully and drill deep into your market so you can become an expert within it. I admire champion sportspeople, gold medal winners, and cup winners. They've specialised, they've become experts in their field. Just watch them on "Question of Sport" when the compère asks if they want home or away questions. They always opt for home and often get the question right. They're experts in their field.

3. Become an expert

Become an expert on the issues surrounding your target market. This is possible if you take an interest in what's going on around you. Read the right blogs, attend the perfect conferences, speak at industry events, hang around online with the right LinkedIn Groups, write for industry publications, be at the forefront of developments, aware of what's coming over the horizon.

Master online research capabilities for your market to ensure you learn about your potential clients and their challenges. Online is where it's at: LinkedIn Group discussions, relevant website discussions, available podcasts, advanced Google search methods, Google Alerts. RSS all the relevant blogs, subscribe to important YouTube Channels, Companies House data, Jigsa.com membership, relevant industry webinars, Slide Share channels, book review sites. If you don't recognise some of these places, you ought to.

4. Ferociously develop content

Ferociously develop content that displays your expertise in your market. The threshold is when you begin to develop your own content that reflects your thinking, not copying everyone else's. When you become insightful, challenge status quo with your advanced thinking, and you can evolve solutions to challenges. Learn how to distribute this content in its multimedia forms – video, podcasts, blogs, articles – place it around the internet for your customers to find when they begin to seek solutions using Google – because they will use Google and find someone else unless you appear in their search.

5. Develop pre-emptive selling skills

Develop the techniques and skills to be able to relate to the people within your markets, namely the analytical skills, coaching skills and customer focus skills.

Analytical skills

Here you need to be good at analysing issues, challenges, and data of your targeted client segment. If you want to pre-empt by launching in early with solutions to perceived problems, you have to have completed your homework on the company. Being able to identify risks to the business, diagnosing the root cause of their current challenge or problem, being able to present complete solutions and calculate the return on investment are all vital capabilities.

Coaching skills

No one wants to be told what to do, especially potential customers. However you have to challenge them, make them think, offer new insights, sometimes unique ones, educate the people surrounding your customer and help them think of the solutions - all in a coaching helping style.

Customer focus skills

The ability to get to know people, show patience for this to happen, being easy to work with, flexible, considering the needs of your customer, understanding them as a person, rapport and empathy building capabilities go without saying. And you need to be accessible, be available in every way the customer prefers – be that Skype, Instant Messaging, email, phone or face to face.

6. Take action

Probably most crucial; the ability to take action. Do all the stages above and then contact your customer, make the phone call without putting it off, agree a meeting following 14 attempts to contact them, have a cosy relationship with their voice mail system and an intimate knowledge of their PA. Earn the right to enter their world with your compelling arguments.

These are the key steps to engage with your customers using a pre-emptive selling philosophy.

Returning to my nuclear holocaust, naturally it never happened and the cold war ended in 1989, with huge relief from all parties especially me hiding under the table. But the rule still applies. He who engages early will win and I'm not thinking of a war situation, just a strategy to help you keep abreast with the changing world dominated by the internet.

No Nonsense Inside Sales

Incubate…Sell…Repeat

It's like distilling brandy

I've always been rather partial to a cheeky drop of brandy or Cognac so I was thrilled when my father emigrated to France and bought a tiny fisherman's cottage near Cognac in the heart of France.

That's where they make the stuff and they're so proud of their process, you can book tours around the breweries to figure out how it works.

Naturally this was the first thing I did on visiting my father's house.

And it was fascinating but boiled down to 3 factors that have a direct correlation to prospecting for the busy professional adviser.

- Firstly they distil the wine, turning the liquid into vapour before allowing it to return to liquid fully distilled.

- Secondly they do this twice to enhance the flavour.

- Thirdly, it takes an absolute age to complete the process.

I'll show you how this relates.

The prospecting engine

So let me share with you the prospecting engine that will ensure you never run out of new business for your professional advisory role. This engine works whatever knowledge you sell. Financial, legal, insurance, management, sales, architectural, accountancy...it doesn't matter so long as you sell your expertise to solve client problems.

The engine works expertly without taking up unnecessary time but you need to invest one day a week on it. No more and no less otherwise you won't be doing much client business. The good news is that once you start it, much of the operation becomes automatic so it's operational even when you are with clients, whilst you sleep and on vacation.

It doesn't involve hard sell although you mustn't forget to sell. Many professionals get lured into the content marketing dream because they're reticent to actually sell. Selling is merely closing and you have to level with yourself what you are actually selling to new clients.

If you don't have a rock solid belief in the value you bring to clients, then the engine won't work since you'll be selling something you don't believe in. This mind-set is essential especially with referral management and making appointment calls.

The last century way to prospect

Back in the day, and I'm talking the 1980s when I started out in financial advisory sales, we had this concept called the sales funnel. Throw prospects into the top of the funnel en masse and gradually you would filter them down by qualifying and you'd end up with motivated clients. It was exhausting and involved lots of cold calling and knocking on doors. Marketing departments would advertise for you and this would put a large clump of new prospects into the funnel. It was essentially a sales driven activity.

But the world has changed. We know that and the facts don't need discussing here. What is clear is that your prospective new clients are in control now and determine the pace of your prospecting.

So we turn the funnel upside down to attract prospects when they want to come in, usually in dribs and drabs rather than en masse. Hence the narrow spout at the top which only allows people in one at a time. I'll talk about what to do once they're in, in a moment, but for now, let's focus on how to get prospects to enter your funnel at the narrow end.

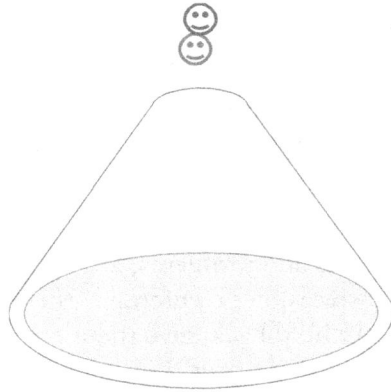

How they get into your incubator

You can't force them in, they must enter voluntarily, so they need a compelling reason to come and join your incubator. And the reason is they want some of your expertise and wish to hang around with you. So you promise this if they enter.

The most traditional route is via a website sign up form. In return for your expertise, your prospect provides you with their name and email address. And they're in. Many professionals will store these people in some form of auto responder email programme from the likes of Mailchimp. These firms make it dead easy to email your expertise on a regular basis but they don't allow just everyone in. Only people who have opted in. You see they're paranoid about people accusing them of sending out spam so only allow people onto the list who have asked to be there.

But if you think about it, these people want your expertise and may, one day, buy something from you. But that comes much later; right now we're merely incubating them.

You can manually add people to your upside-down funnel from a variety of sources, just don't put them into your email programme. Harvested business cards, previous clients, audiences who have given you their names, your LinkedIn connections, product buyers, Twitter followers, Facebook friends.

The differentiator is that they are only browsing. They don't want to talk to you, don't want to buy your expertise, they're just interested in it and are quite happy to consume the free stuff you provide. One day they might be ready to buy from you, possibly never. I've had prospects in my upside down funnel for over 15 years; some of them have never bought anything, but love to consume my expertise.

I'll talk about hot prospects shortly.

Keeping your incubator warm

Over time, your incubator will fill with people who are interested in what you do, so now you have to give them what they want – your expertise. How you do this is for another day to discuss and everyone has their favourites when it comes to content creation. Because you are an expert, a professional who sells expertise, you just create content that your audiences want to consume in ways that suit them.

Create content that solves their pains and problems, answers questions your audiences might have, helps them in their goals, inspires them, entertains them. Produce material that clearly demonstrates your expertise. Don't hold back, give them everything, after all the internet can and does provide everything they will ever need.

Your role, or it should be, is to use your expertise and tailor solutions to individual clients. The materials they consume are "off the shelf" solutions, not the bespoke application of your expertise that you charge a fee for.

Blogs, YouTube Channels, Vimeo Channels, articles, regular columns, White Papers, Web Meetings, telephone seminars, eBooks, Twitter feeds, LinkedIn Pulse articles, article websites, Facebook posts. You can direct people to your content using the mail system that you use. Links, downloads. Just feed everyone in your incubator with regular, multi-sensory, compelling content.

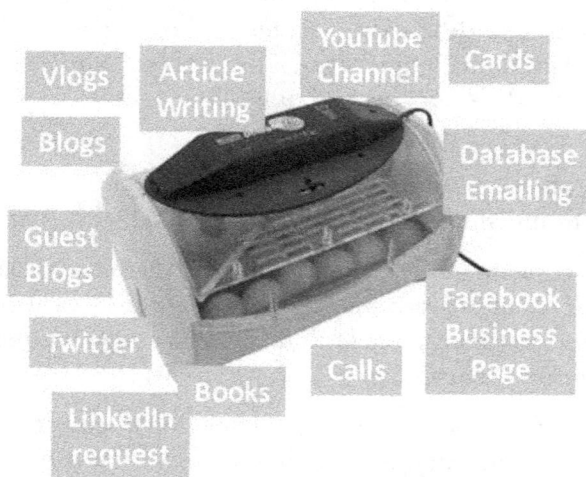

You're not selling, you're incubating

Why can't I sell to the people in my incubator, after all, I need to make a living? I hear you cry. Of course you can and many experts do, sprinkling their posts with adverts and calls to action. My view on this is that you will put more people off than attract clients. Remember they are in charge, not you, it's their buying process that we want to latch onto and when they're ready, they'll slip through and reach out.

And that's the next step. Have a look at the diagram below and you'll see our incubator keeps people hovering, but when they want to they can drop below into the more traditional sales funnel. If you look closely, there's also a side-entrance, which I'll explain.

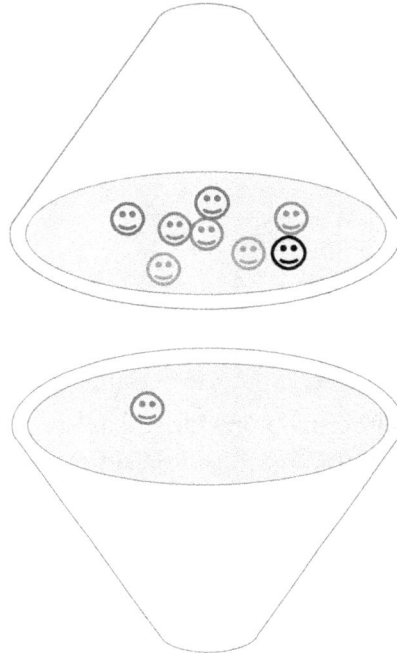

From incubator to the sales funnel

So far we've been talking about gradually filling up your incubator over time using expertise in the form of content to lure them in. Over time, they'll come to see you as the person who can solve their needs, so they'll drop out of the incubator into your sales funnel and this is where the fun starts. Unfortunately, this is the bit many professional advisers forget or leave out of their marketing. I think many of us have forgotten to sell as we've been rendered drunk by the lore of content marketing which doesn't have any rejection. The sales funnel we're about to explore has rejection in it…lots.

Take the side entrance

Back to the side entrance. This is where you manually enter "hot" prospects to receive the intense treatment. These people are ready to buy, need their pain solved, have a budget to pay for it and may already have heard about you. Those dropping out of the incubator already know you're the "go to" person, the side entrance is for new entrants.

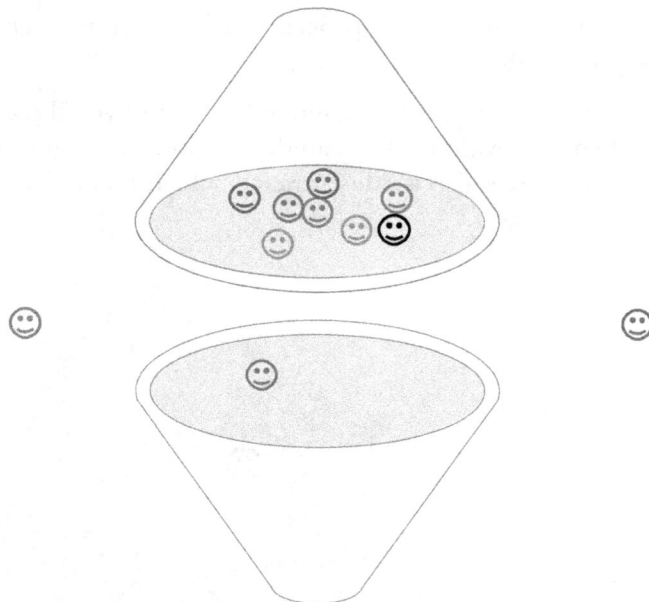

For me, it's referred prospects either from my client base or my network of friends/colleagues. About 50% of my new business comes from this source and once they're provided to me, I have to act quickly. Other people here might be those who made a direct contact with you – phone, email, tweet, text – they found you on the web and need to talk to you quickly.

It could be a bought lead that you've purchased. My accountant secured my business in this way. I reached out to an accountancy forum for local accountants a couple of years ago and the forum charged local accountants to make contact with me. He paid them, contacted me and the rest is history.

A LinkedIn PQC

I manually insert other "hot" leads in here. One major source of new business for me is LinkedIn and if you're a professional selling your expertise, it probably is important for you too. Here's how it works:

I place my LinkedIn profile button everywhere and encourage all those who find me on the internet and offline as well to link in with me. Many people are precious about who they will link in with and that's fine. If someone makes a request to link in, if they are in my industry sector (which is professional services expertise sellers), I email them and ask to arrange a 10 minute telephone conversation so I can explore their role, goals and challenges.

It's amazing how effective this is. Firstly LinkedIn emails get opened. Secondly, around 75% of people agree to the call usually rescheduling to a time that's more convenient. During the call, if there's synergy, we talk further. I have secured some important new contracts with this prospecting method as it's a non-sales exploratory phone call which allows me to pitch if there's a connection.

I call this a PQC – prospect qualifying call

Your selling process

From now on, for a salesperson like me, it gets exciting because you're doing a deal. Prospects that fall into the traditional funnel need special attention. You have incubated prospects who know you, like you, trust you since they've been subjected to your online content expertise for a while, sometimes years.

You have LinkedIn requests from potential clients who you've scoped out and realise they have a need you can help with, you have referred prospects who are looking for you to solve a problem or pain they have. You also have prospects who have reached out to you pro-actively so they have a need that desires solving.

You have to action these; don't expect the sale to drop in your lap, you need to make contact some way and move them along your selling steps, as we used to call our sales process. Here's how I do it for my business.

I have a CRM system that manages all this for me, naturally, so should you. Which one is up for debate, they all do what they say. You should look for one that stores the data in the cloud and has access via your Smartphone or tablet.

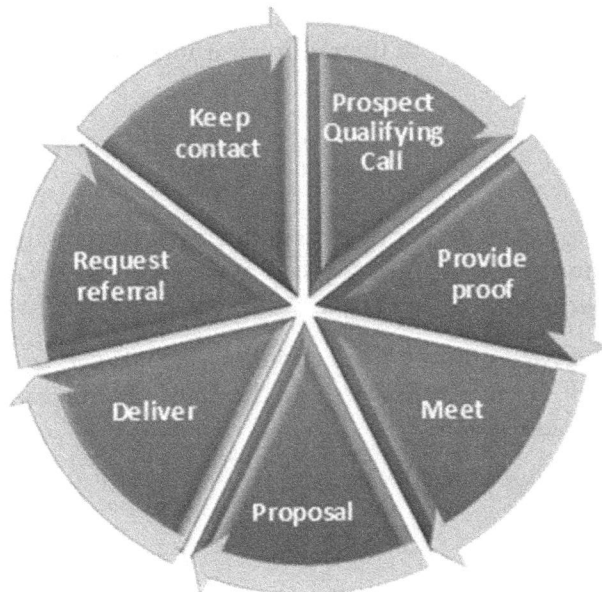

I also have a giant whiteboard in my office which I use to write down the progress of my "hot" pipeline. What you can see gets done.

My sales steps start with a contact. Not email but a face to face or voice to voice one. Email is 1D, phone is 2D but face to face is 3D. 3D requires you spend your dollar going to see the customer. You could do Skype. I'm skyping someone later this month who lives in Indonesia – I live in the UK.

This requires that you make an appointment call or email. Calls are better with referrals. Learn how to make effective appointment calls; it's a science as well as an art.

This contact allows you to explore the needs of your prospect, discover pains and problems, lets you talk about your expertise and how you might be able to provide a solution.

In the meantime I bombard them with evidence to prove my expertise. I might send a copy of one of my books, a link to a YouTube video on my channel, a White Paper – often printed and posted – adding them to my email list, Linking In with them. The purpose here is to provide proof of expertise, which is an essential element to trust.

The "hot" prospects in my traditional funnel take some time. This should be done immediately wherever you are in the world. This week I'm out to Dhaka and doing a Skype call in the middle of the week. Just because you're busy doesn't stop your prospecting.

Following an exploratory meeting, my next step is some form of proposal which I always deliver in person on Skype. Never, ever just post it and pray. PIAP – post it and pray – destroys the confidence of more knowledgeable professionals than I care to mention.

Negotiate and close...do the work...put them into your incubator.

Incubate...sell....repeat.

Back to brandy

And to my brandy analogy. Remember they distil the wine, turning the liquid into vapour before allowing it to return to liquid fully distilled as brandy. And it takes an age to complete but the end result is pure gold.

Your incubator can keep someone warm for months, years. It can take an age for the prospect to filter through but when they do, and drop into the sales process part of the funnel, it can turn into gold for you.

After all this hard work, I think I need a brandy!

Prospecting Under Scrutiny

No "Cold Call" B2B Prospecting

Let me show you step by step how to leverage LinkedIn to make contacts with people you've never met before and get right through to the decision maker.

Ingredients

1. A trigger point that is causing a company some pain

2. LinkedIn Premium

3. Targeted customers i.e. companies plus title of person with pain, e.g. sales director

Method

1. Jot down the magic email, i.e. the pain you feel the prospect is suffering, how you can fix the pain, why you're good at this and what others say and finally, a simple and easy call to action.

2. Into LinkedIn, ensuring you've signed up for the premium service, head to "advanced search".

3. In the advanced search box, key in the company's name and the title of the person you want to contact.

4. From the response, sift through until you find the person's LinkedIn profile, the premium version lets you look at their entire profile not just snippets. Ensure it is the right person in the company.

5. Make a note as to who is jointly connected, i.e. which of your LinkedIn connections is also connected to them, a second is best.

6. Click on "InMail". This is a really neat feature of LinkedIn premium and allows you to send an email using the LinkedIn engine. The prospect receives an email from LinkedIn which has been proven to have a much higher incidence of being opened.

7. Copy your magic email from earlier. The subject line must be the problem/pain you think they're suffering with. Ensure you drop in the email who is jointly connected, for example "I notice that you're also connected to Vinay Patel, he

and I have known each other for 10 years". Put this at the end of the paragraph that describes your proof of being able to solve the problem.

8. Repeat this 10 or so times for the companies that you wish to target. It takes a little longer than cold emails, which rarely work – they rarely even get through without being deleted - so it's worth doing, but it's best to be selective at first.

9. Leave to simmer for 2 days and await the results. Because the call to action is easy, i.e. ping back this email with your phone number and I'll give you a call, it works well.

10. Rejoice in the fact that your prospects will respond, some saying no thanks, and that's fine, but some will come back and say, "Yes we have a need there and it might be useful to talk".

You've successfully caught them at the beginning of their buying process as they've developed an itch and will seek out a scratch. And you're there early on providing that scratch.

Getting in early has many advantages. You can serve them earlier to build some loyalty, impress them so they don't need to go elsewhere or even lay some landmines which you know your competitors can't contest with.

Real-world Example

Last weekend an associate of mine alerted me to the fact that secured loan companies, those who sell secured loans to customers direct, are to be regulated in the same manner as mortgage advisers.

The deadline is March 2016 and today is July 2015. Clearly these companies will have an itch which my company can scratch for them.

Yesterday I made a list of the companies who provide second charge lending, both lenders and brokers. This is easy enough to find on the internet and took me 30 minutes. I had 20 companies.

Then I opened up LinkedIn. I knew from memory 3 of the companies I had dealings with already, so a quick search of the people already LinkedIn with me brought up their profile and a personal LinkedIn email was sent to these people, along the lines of the magic email, but with much more customisation such as their partner's name and how had they been keeping.

These got me a 100% response later that day, which you would expect.

Then I tickled LinkedIn for her own magic and using advanced search, quickly found the sales director of the next company. Remember it's the person who owns the pain you want. Yes, they may delegate it to their training manager or compliance manager, but delegation has never shed the responsibility. Besides they hold the budget, usually not training managers who often spend other peoples'.

I sent the InMails, carefully copying my magic email, and making a reference to the jointly connected people on our profiles and I left an easy call to action:

Merely respond to this email with your number and I'll phone you.

I sent around 10 InMails altogether.

The results? Still coming in as we speak. I had an out and out rejection, and that's fine, LinkedIn refunds my InMail. This morning I had a response from a CEO and she asked me to phone her. She gave me a number and we agreed a telephone meeting on Monday morning when she was less harassed. She is keen to bring someone in to help her. Well worth a telephone call.

This afternoon, I had another response who mentioned that one of my existing clients from the earlier list had contacted them to say that Paul Archer might be able to help in this matter.

It's amazing how existing clients are willing to provide referrals if we ask them. Coupled with the recommendation and the InMail, he now also wants me to phone him to have a conversation.

And we're only at day two. But it's Friday now, closing on 5pm, so I'm going to close the office door, head to the sunny patio and enjoy a well-earned glass of wine.

PS. LinkedIn Premium also gives you the ability to look at everyone who's checked your profile. If they're in my sector, I always send a LinkedIn request along the lines of; I noticed you called by, let's connect and chat at your leisure. Once we've connected I send a LinkedIn email to see if they would want 10 minutes to talk about their business. This almost always works and I really do just listen to them and their business.

Acquiring new clients

Back in the day my client acquisition method was the Phone Book and Yellow Pages. I'm sure none of you remember those and my first day in the insurance business was pure cold calling. Hard knocks and tiring.

Then came family and friends when I was asked to "tap" up my network for referrals, this was more successful. But things became far easier when I was plopped into an estate agency branch in the High Street so I could feed from the leads provided by the guys at the front office.

Of course times have changed. No longer can we cold call nor do we want to. Our industry has accelerated to become one of the professional and with this rise in stature, comes more advanced methods of gaining new business.

Busy financial advisers tend to work with about 4 methods nowadays:

Referrals, by far the most professional technique from clients and contacts in the industry such as accountants. This method can feed you with non-competitive and long lasting client relationships. By far my favourite.

Then comes leads either bought from the internet or provided by your office.

Finally comes contact with past clients known as orphan clients. People who haven't heard from you or your company in some while and who may have forgotten about you.

There are very few other methods that truly work, apart of course, from a strong existing relationship with your client who continues to look to you for professional financial advice.

The need to call

All of these methods of attracting new clients require a further step though. You need to contact them to fix up an initial meeting. Email is only 1 dimensional and often leads to failure with the prevalence of spam traps and easy delete keys, so it leaves us to phone instead.

But picking up the phone with someone you don't know and haven't met can create a sense of doom with many financial advisers so I'm going to give you some ideas on how you can do this successfully.

Preparation

Just like a good decorator. We had a guy in recently to decorate and after two days slaving at work I couldn't see a lick of paint. He was preparing.

So what preparation do we need to do?

The first piece of preparation is to get it clear in your head as to the value you provide since you're going to have to articulate this when, and if, you get through to your new customer. Bear in mind if it's a lead, either bought and paid for or collected from a referral source such as an existing client or associate arrangement, they won't know you and may not be totally aware of how you work and the value you provide. And the orphan client you're phoning may well have forgotten totally who you are and how you now work.

The 7 questions to ask yourself to know your value

Ask yourself the following 7 questions:

1. Who am I?
2. What do I do?

3.   Why do I do what I do?

4.   How do I do what I do?

5.   Whom have I performed services for?

6.   What makes me different from other advisers?

7.   Why should clients do business with me?

Have a trusted friend ask you the questions in a coaching style, audio record the answers you give and transcribe these into a value proposition or elevator pitch or sound bite. It doesn't matter what you call it, just get it clear, succinct and valuable.

Then carry out some belief change work if you still don't believe in your value. Email me and I'll suggest some belief change exercises for you and some assertion work. Whatever we do, you simply have to be your own number one fan.

Motivation

The next piece of preparation is to get you up and motivated to make these calls especially if you have a few to do. Let me be upfront and personal on this, most financial advisers I know, do not look forward to making these calls because they invite a "no".

You see as a child you did everything possible to avoid the dreaded "no". With your parents, your teachers, family…the last thing you wanted to hear was "no", so you avoided it at all costs. That same trait continued into your grown up years and exists today.

So you have to get over it.

There's various things you can do and there's a time and a place for it.

The time comprises of how many calls you need to make and the right time to call. Depending on how many calls you need to make will determine how long you spend but it's known that no more than 45 minutes of calling is desirable. Beyond that and you go flat.

The key is to sit down, or stand up, in a private place to make the calls. Don't be interrupted in making the calls, make them one after the other because you get into a routine and the time flows quickly.

How many calls should you make? Well that depends on how you work. Those that make these kind of calls for a living work with activity ratios or funnels as we used to call them. They've figured out that if they need 1 appointment, then normally they have to speak with at least 3 people, and to get through to 3 people they need to make 10 calls or dials. So they figure 45 minutes is enough time to get 20 calls done, which will let them get through and speak with 6 people, and they'll make 2 appointments. Not bad for 45 minutes' work.

Golden rules to making calls

That's the time, next the place. Here's a couple of golden rules when making these calls:

1. Try and arrange calls in batches and make an easy call to start with.

2. Don't stop what you're doing and prevent interruptions.

3. Make notes directly onto the CRM you're using rather than leaving it for later.

4. Remember you're making appointments, not selling.

5. Try and get straight onto the next call after each call.

6. Have a standard response to voice-mail, no tricks, just state you'll call back another time.

7. Call during standard blocks – 9 to 11am; 4 to 6pm; and 7pm to 8pm actually works.

Voice mail

Before we get into your call structure a final word about voice mail and how to leave one.

I'm very busy as are you but my world consists of very long meetings which can last all day without much time to eat let alone return calls. So when I do, I usually take about 4 or 5 calls all at once. And that's the point. Voice mail is linear, you listen to the first one, then delete, then the second and delete. Rarely do we go back and listen again.

So start your voice mail with your name and number then leave your reason for them to call back, then leave your name and number at the end because few people note it down at the beginning and aren't likely to rewind the voice mail. Tape based voice mail machines went out in the 1990s.

Call structure

The final piece of preparation is your call structure or call process. Yes, you need this, you can't wing it. We're going to look at the bullets of a structure that actually work and still give you the freedom to free-wheel a little and sound human, not like some cold calling canvasser.

Here's the steps and I'll talk about each in turn:

1. Intro

2. Sound bite

3. Ask for appointment

4. Close

The intro allows you to check the person who's speaking and use their name a couple of times.

The sound bite is your opportunity to give your reason for calling and the value potentially you can give the customer. You need to get them interested straight away.

If it's a referral, say something like, "Has Bob Monkhouse mentioned my name to you recently and that I'd be calling?" or, "Your accountant, Bob Monkhouse has asked me to give you a call."

If it's an orphan client say something like, "GBD Consultancy in the High Street have asked me to call you about the business you've done with them recently."

If it's following a letter, say something like, "I'm calling regarding the letter we sent you this week, did you receive it?"

If it's a bought lead, say something like, "You've just been online and wanted a financial specialist to call."

At this point you want to hear their reaction and now give your value or sound bite. Which of course is what you honed earlier, didn't you?

Say something like, "GBD have recently developed a new service to help clients understand the new pensions rules and we'd like the opportunity to speak with you about them to see if we can help you retire more comfortably" or,

"GBD have designed a new service to help you mortgage or remortgage your home at vastly lower interest rates" or,

"GBD have been working with clients recently helping them to grown their investments in the current low interest environment".

Or whatever the sound bite is that you've created for the call.

Again, get their reaction.

Now take control and ask for a meeting to discuss.

"I'm setting up new client meetings here in the office for next week and I have Monday evening or Saturday morning available. Which would suit?"

It's inertia that you're looking for to agree a meeting time. Try not to get involved in a long conversation about your service. Keep coming back to the point that it's best if we meet face to face, it's a complimentary initial explore meeting to see if we can be a fit, I've opened my client bank up to accept some new clients which is why we thought to phone you…or whatever works to secure the meeting.

Agree the time, thank them for their time and then follow up with a letter or email, whichever you use. And do remember to call them just before the allotted time to share with them how the meeting will work, to remind them to bring in various items and to confirm where to park the car. I used to take their tea order during this pre-call too.

Handling reservations

Initial reservations. Back in the day we would encourage learning how to overcome every objection known and had some serious techniques for swinging the customer around to your way of thinking. How times have changed, thankfully.

Try and put yourself in the customer's shoes. They vaguely recall your company or you and they're truly rather busy. How would you like it if some pushy financial adviser was trying to get an appointment from you?

No, instead accept graciously their initial "no"; this is often a knee jerk reaction. Show empathy for their position but if you truly believe in the service and value you give your clients, repeat this value and ask for another convenient time to talk. You'll be surprised, by accepting their initial "no" but merely repeating your value with a voice of surprise, will often win them over.

Now most people you deal with are going to be consumers, rich or poor. But some of you may be calling on small business owners or orphan clients at work so you may have to work doubly hard to actually get through to them especially if they have good voice mail and a loyal personal assistant who has the motto "no-one gets through".

Here's some ideas that might work in these situations.

- Call out of hours; say before 9am and during lunch time. Often her PA is not at her desk so you'll actually get the person you want answering the phone.

- Use the phrase, "My company has asked me to call Mike". For example "GDA Consulting has asked me to contact Mike Brown, is he there please?"

- Make it very casual, for example "Hiya, Mike please, it's Brian for him".

- Make the PA your ally. Explain that you need their help to speak with Mike and be really polite.

- Or just phone them at home or on their mobile.

Regular calling

I firmly believe that all businesses need an element of new business, and new clients since there'll always be a need. My wife keeps chickens and ducks. At last count we had over 15 of them pecking away in the field next to our house yet each year my wife brings in some new chicks or fertilised eggs to add to her flock. I was bemused so I asked her why. Her response was that each year she'll lose some hens. Some to illness, some to old age and some to the wily old fox. So adding new ones each spring just means she keeps the same number.

Clever really, and that's exactly why you need to keep adding new customers to your client bank. You'll lose some through natural causes, defections and the competition maybe…so always be adding to your flock.

Principles of Making Appointments

Chain yourself to your desk for 45 minutes

On Sunday mornings I referee mini rugby matches for my son's rugby club. Now being a referee isn't a recipe for compliments and lovely words from players, coaches and spectators. Sometimes it's quite the opposite, so why do I do it? Well it's certainly not for the feel good warm and snuggly feelings! But doing a good job can be gratifying and it keeps me fit.

Likewise making calls to fix up appointments isn't something every salesperson wants to do because you'll get your fair share of refusals and no's. And these don't engender warm snuggly feelings. It's not a pleasurable task. And it doesn't keep you fit either.

So the trick is to chain yourself to your desk for 45 minutes and do nothing else but make calls otherwise it's very easy to be distracted to another gratifying task such as checking email or making a cup of tea.

45 minutes is shown to be the optimum timing for making calls – any shorter and you won't get through the calls you have to make, any longer and you begin to lose your sharpness and enthusiasm.

Many salespeople ask me what is the best time to make the calls. That depends much on your body clock and when you think your prospects will be in to receive your call. It's known that between 9 to 11am is the most effective time. Next is 7 to 8pm and the worst time is between 4 to 6pm.

The days you decide to make your calls must fit around your schedule although we have found Fridays to not be as successful as say a Tuesday, as people have an "end of the week" feeling.

Sellotape the phone to your wrist

This principle leads on from the last one with the overriding concern being how easily distracted salespeople are (and I put myself in that category as well). The rule to follow is the 60 second rule. When you've hung up on the customer, keep the phone in your hand for a maximum of 60 seconds before you make your next outgoing call.

Not only does this prevent you taking an incoming call but it stops you doing much else apart from making important notes or diary entries with your other hand. Use your left hand to hold the receiver thus freeing up your writing hand unless you're left handed of course.

Use a hands free device as you'll never be tempted to cradle the receiver in your neck. Not good.

Use a stop watch if you like.

And don't be tempted to use a conference facility on your phone so you can use both hands. They differ in quality so ensure you get to take a call from someone else using conference facilities to test the quality of your system. Some sound as though you're in the rest room and some have a mini second of silence between you talking and the other person talking which doesn't sound natural.

Do not disturb

Next time you're in a hotel, grab the "do not disturb" sign and use this when you enter your 45 minutes of calling. Hang it on your back to warn prospective interrupters not to disturb you. Explain to everyone in the office or workplace that you need 45 minutes of uninterrupted time to make your appointments, so can they hold calls and messages until afterwards.

Ensure you have everything to hand before you pick up the phone and start your stopwatch. CRM package opened up, diary ready and pen that works with some note paper ready. And remember to switch off your mobile phone as well.

Know what it is you sell

A little obvious but worth reminding yourself of what it is you are aiming to achieve with the call. You're after a meeting either face to face or maybe via web conferencing or telephone. You do not want to be sucked into discussing the product or service.

Focus on getting the appointment and you'll be successful.

But you do need to motivate the prospect to want to meet up with you and here you need to know what their motivation is. WIIFM – or what's in it for me. What is it that the prospect will buy into – what's the hook or hot button?

Keep the hook enticing and leave out the detail. Make the prospect feel hungry but don't feed them. For a financial services call, it might be to save them money, provide security for the future or secure the best finance for them. These sound interesting but don't go into detail.

When probed for more information, explain that this is why meeting them face to face is advantageous to you both and you'll be happy to do this for them. Repeat the hot buttons once more.

Plan don't can

In every aspect of selling we follow the golden rule of plan, do, and review. Plan your calling. Some salespeople like to follow a script and this is fine so long as the words are natural and not canned. Unfortunately scripted written words just don't always sound right when spoken. For example:

"Can I just spend 5 minutes of your time to explain..."

Sounds very formal but I've seen it on hundreds of scripts. Instead use:

"Could I just walk you through..."

Or something similar.

Whether you script or not you do need a plan to follow. The 4 essentials to a successful calling plan are; introduction, ice breaker, reason for the call and asking for the appointment. You do need some clear words and scripts within each heading and here are some ideas and pointers for you.

Scripting your prospecting call

Not too much polish is the key, a polished call doesn't fit. It feels out of place with today's savvy customers. Let me explain and give you some ideas to help.

Every Sunday night I polish my family's shoes in preparation for the next day's school and work. I think shiny polished shoes are the epitome of smartness. But by Monday night, the children's shoes have deteriorated into mud strewn, scratched and dented specimens and bear little resemblance to my Sunday efforts.

So why bother? I like them to go to school looking smart and polished but school soon knocks them into shape. My youngest son Euan even admitted to deliberately scuffing them. Asked why, he replied they looked odd, different and he didn't fit in, so he scuffed them.

That's school for you. Polishing doesn't fit in. But what about telephone prospecting calls? Should they be polished? No, if you want to fit in, in the same manner with my school shoes, they will look and sound odd and out of place.

So I ask you to un-polish your scripts and make them sound like real phrases and sentences you would normally use. You know, ones that we speak, ones where we pause suddenly and "uhm" every now and then. Sentences that you could imagine come from a human rather than a computer generated recorded message. Sound normal.

The key is write how you speak. If you find this difficult, then record your script onto your computer and play it back at the same time, then type it up. Use a free service on the internet that transcribes the spoken word into type. Just type it out, leave out punctuation, pauses, sentences.

And then when you practise the words, put in your normal pauses, uhms, stutters, etc. Try not to be too polished as this can quickly be heard and it turns customers off who think you sound like a cold calling merchant.

But I will continue to polish the family's shoes on a Sunday night. One must have one's principles you know.

Outbound Call Structure

A very impressive cold call

This morning I happened to be particularly busy, lots of "to do" jobs, some deadlines, challenges to consider and a few calls from clients expected. Then the office phone rang.

It wasn't the client I was expecting; it was Bob from a local stationery supplier.

Bob was impressive, I mean good, real, genuine and his call worked.

The odd thing is that I normally give cold callers a Paul Archer bark as soon as I get the "Is that Mr Archer?" or the ubiquitous "Is it convenient to call?"

No, Bob was notable because he'd done his homework before calling me. He knew my name, and was happy to call me by my first name Paul, after all this is the 21st Century, not the late Victorian age. He knew I was local and had a need to buy stationery and he figured I was looking for good prices from this commodity.

In other words he'd done some qualifying. Afterwards I asked him how he did this. He said simple. He looked up my name under training organisations using yell.com, got my first name, Googled me, checked out my LinkedIn profile and 123people.com and within 2 minutes he knew quite a lot about me. Scary eh?

But the cleverest thing about Bob's technique was his ability to get into my shoes and appreciate that his call was going to interrupt me, stop me from doing what I was doing before he called. He therefore got to the point quickly and effectively. I liked that. And his close was exceptional.

"Is it a good time to talk further now Paul or shall we schedule another call for later." I asked him to phone back later that day, which he did and for which he had my full attention.

His hook was carefully thought out, prepared and relevant to my expected needs.

"We've got some cracking deals on stationery for local businesses like yours, Paul"

And the best bit was he got straight to the point. No "How are you?" or "Is it ok to call you Paul?", no, he just got to the point, gave me a fab sound bite or hook, spoke clearly, not too fast with an enthusiastic tone.

He was clear as to his goal for the call. He wanted me to head over to the local store in Cheltenham, I guess they're drumming up walk in trade from local small businesses and the value of the discount voucher he promised me made my eyes water.

So when I asked about the cracking deals, he told me about one but kept to his guns and carried on persuading me to head to the store saying the deals were exclusively available there and I'd need to head over to benefit from them.

Bob's strategy

So if you're in the business of making calls to customers, just follow Bob's strategy.

1. Do brief research on your customer to make sure they are a fit.

2. Perk up your voice and get excited.

3. Get straight to the point, no tricks or "how are you's?"

4. Use a sound bite that bites and tailor this to your customer's needs.

5. Stick to your guns and know what you want to get from the call and ask for this. Then shut up.

6. Overcome the objection by reasserting what you want.

7. Appreciate that the person you're calling is busy and you've interrupted them. Imagine how they feel.

Well done Bob, you got my business.

An ideal structure

Here we have the structure which I've identified makes the difference between being successful in making appointments with the modern buyer.

The first point to make here is that whatever your lead, the process is the same. The prospect may be a referral, a networking lead, a cold call…it doesn't really matter as long as the appointment making process is concerned. But naturally a referral or one where there is a relationship already, is much easier and more than likely to end in a successful appointment.

Research

It's all to do with research. What's the "hook", in other words the reason for your call, and it's not to make an appointment. Yes that's the objective, but not the reason to call.

The hook is the value statement that you're going to be giving them which relates to the trigger event and the pain and the solution that you can talk about.

Open the Call

Once you get put through to your prospect and this is actually quite an achievement these days, you need to sound non-scripted, unpolished. The last thing you want here is to be immediately spotted as a cold caller. "Not another sales call!" Urgggg.

Value Statement

Come in quickly with your value statement, designed to solve their problems, refer to the trigger event maybe. Talk quickly about cost saving, time saving, profit increase, revenue rise.

Some people call this the Sound Bite.

Let the value of what you do come over in a few sentences.

Do it quickly, clearly and then get a reaction.

Question

You need to test close here by getting a reaction.

"Is it OK to talk now, or shall we schedule a call later?" works sometimes, especially if you sense they're very busy.

"How relevant Richard, is this to you right now?"

"How much value is there in talking about this further?"

Have some planned questions to find out about them and their situation. Don't leave it to chance, plan your questions.

Some people like to hit the mute button after a questions to stop them butting in. Be careful of the impression this may leave, so check your technology.

Close

Suggest the objective, which is to talk further. It might be another call, it might be an appointment for you or your account manager to call. Take control and suggest the next step.

Never ever, leave this open. Always have a next step.

The Appointment Template

Intro

(Name)......................................Please

Thank you.

(Name)...........this is........................from............................. How are you today?

Ice Breaker

Referral	"Has (referrer)........mentioned my name to you at all recently?"
Orphan	"(Company)...........has asked me to call you about.............................."
Letter	"This call is regarding the letter we sent you. Did you receive it?"
Cold	"Has my name been mentioned to you at all recently?"

Fine. The reason for the call today (name)..................as you may be aware is that
(company)..................has recently developed a (service/idea/plan) designed to

(Hot buttons)

For people like you and we'll be happy to give you the opportunity of seeing it.

Ask for Appointment

I'm calling (name)........to say that I'll be in your area/able to set up a telephone meeting
on.............and wondered would you be available at that time.

When would suit you?

Objections

That's OK (name)....... I do see how you feel about that and I must say lots of our clients
Have felt the same way like you. But once they get to sit down/talk to us further, they've
Found that the time was very valuable to them. I wonder when would suit you?

That's OK (name)....... We find that this is the case with most people even before we ring.
My call today is only to ask the courtesy of a meeting to outline this (idea/plan/concept) to you
So that if you're interested in the future you'll know what's available.
I'm in your area/able to set up a telephone meeting on and wondered would you be
available at that time?

Working with Voicemail

Voicemail is linear

It's been hot this week, and travelling around the country in planes, trains and automobiles takes its toll. But nothing is more strenuous than picking up voicemail.

I pick up voicemail at the end of the day, as I never get the chance during the day. This week I've been phoning in using my mobile phone to listen to my office messages, which a lot of road warriors do. And I get the same frustrations every time.

I listen and the lady with BBC English from BT Call Minder announces I have 5 messages, so I hit 1 to play and listen to the first one. Didn't quite catch the first name, message sounds interesting though, what was his name and number again? Better save it.

Next message, not interested, key in 3 to delete.

Next message. Crikey, she went on with that message and lost me half way so hit delete. If it's important she'll call back.

This one is important, what was his number? Have to listen all over again. Bother, what was the number to re-listen, 3 wasn't it? Rats, I've just deleted it by mistake.

You see the problem with voice mail is that they're linear, you have to listen to them in order, it's so difficult to re-wind, go forward, repeat if you have a series to listen to. And most people do. Very few of us grab the voicemail as soon as it's come in. No, we listen to them all together.

Here's some tips to help you leave better voicemail.

1. Give your name and number clearly at the beginning.

2. Leave your message, maximum 30 seconds in total.

3. If you want them to call you back, then leave a compelling message with a solid reason why they should call you back. Don't trick or confuse, just make it compelling.

4. At the end, repeat your name and number quickly.

5. Speak slower than you normally do.

6. Finally email the same message immediately afterwards, if you can.

Follow these tips and I bet you that people like me won't delete your message by mistake rather than hitting the rewind button.

Get straight through

Do you what the most annoying modern trend in the world is right now? It's got to be the phone systems that try to direct you to a particular department. There are officially the worst invention ever.

Here's a great tip I heard the other day. When the diatribe starts…just hit 0 or # on the keypad and chances are you'll go straight to the receptionist who'll put you through to your prospect or their gatekeeper.

Are you a Speedy Gonzalez or a Mysterious Professor?

Mysterious Professors, when they leave voicemail messages, often leave out important information which drives the recipients wild with frustration. If you feel you bear a resemblance to the Professor, you will want to make sure you leave a decent message that people can readily understand.

It's a good idea to leave a longer message just in case your request can be dealt with without them phoning you back or packed with some benefits to give them a reason to phone you back.

Ensure that you leave your name and number clearly at both the beginning and the end of the call, spelling your name and repeating your number.

Now Speedy Gonzalez is a different character altogether, always rushing around, busy busy. When they leave messages it's quick and efficient but often too quick for the poor soul trying to decipher the message at the other end.

Whether you are a Speedy or not, we really ought to slow down our rate of speech on voicemail messages.

A good tip is to imagine the other person is writing down the key points of your message as you speak it. That way you will slow down especially at important points.

Be aware that some mobile messages are lost in transmission – maybe a challenging signal area means that not all your message gets through so maybe repeat key information such as your phone number.

A hypnotic voice mail message

Like you, I often get calls from suppliers vying for my business and good luck to them I say. Last week I had a very mysterious message from a car dealer – Mitsubishi here in Cheltenham.

For the last three years they've been trying to get me to part exchange my aging Shogun for a shiny new model and this time they seemed to be trying a new tactic.

It was a voice mail message which went something like this:

"Hello Mr Archer, it's Bob here from Mitsubishi Motors in Cheltenham. I wanted you to be the first to know of an absolutely fantastic offer that we have exclusively for existing owners of Shoguns. We're limiting this special offer to only a few names and since your surname begins with A, you're one of the first people we're phoning. The offer, well it........."

And then it went blank as though he got cut off.

Mmm I thought, what is this offer? I won't be tempted but I'd sure like to know what the offer is. This bugged me all evening and by the morning I was begging for 9am to come by so I could phone Bob…just to see what the offer was.

All very hypnotic.

The moral here is to leave something of interest on your voice mails. The standard

"Hi, it's Paul Archer here, I have some very interesting proposals for you – please phone me back on..."

Just won't work.

Try

"Hi Brian, its Paul Archer from Archer Training. I've been working with other firms in your industry and I have some great ideas that will help you increase your sales revenue. Love to talk these through with you; please can you call me back on…"

Be inspirational with your ideas, use plenty of benefits, leave something of obvious value to your prospect to ensure they call you back.

And no, Bob's offer didn't tempt me to buy a new car, but I was very very tempted.

Some voicemail scripts that work

A great fit

"Hi Prospect's name, this is …. You and I haven't spoken yet, but I've been doing some research on your company and I think you're a great fit for telecoms solutions. We can provide you with (one or two benefits) and I know you'll be happy if we spend just a couple of minutes discussing how this can help you.

When you get this message, please call me back at … That number again is … and ask for … I look forward to speaking with you, and I guarantee you'll be glad you returned this call."

This could work for you

"Hi …this is …Briefly Bob, I need to speak with you about how you're handling your communications, because I have something that can (solve their unique problem). Our clients include (list some companies they are familiar with), and I know this would work for you as well. Believe me it'll be worth a 5 minute phone call to find out why.

Please do me a favour when you get this message and call me back at (Your Number). That number again is (Your Number) and ask for …. I look forward speaking with you and I guarantee you'll be glad you returned this call."

Partnering Gatekeepers

The phonetic alphabet

I recall my children learning the phonetic alphabet at school and I remember reading stories to my daughter all about Annie Apple and Naughty Nick and his lost nails.

Great fun and a useful tip when getting people's names from the gatekeeper is to write the difficult ones down phonetically rather than literally. Type this into your CRM system so when you get to talk to them, you're able to say their name perfectly.

Spell it as it is said, is the key.

A short tip that'll pay you big dividends when you get to pronounce the name of a prospect when everyone else gets it wrong.

Ask for their help

For most salespeople, if not all of us, being nice to people is second nature and something that gives us plenty of pleasure. So being extremely nice to the gatekeeper should come naturally to us.

The problem is we know they have been created to fob us off as their boss doesn't want any sales calls.

And this puts us on our guard and we leave ourselves to the mercy of the gatekeeper's generosity.

The simple answer is to be very nice to them and ask them for their help. People can't resist helping.

- "Hello I need your help…?"
- "What's the best time to reach Bob?"
- "Hello, can you help me please to get a message through to Bob?"

Are just some ways that you can ask for help to get through to your prospect.

And remember to ask their name and remember it for next time.

Sound important

A UCLA survey showed that on the telephone a massive 84% of the message and meaning is derived purely from your voice. This fact deserves a book in its own right but for now I'm asking that you sound important so you can get through the gatekeeper.

Important people have deeper voices and say things in shorter sentences. Their tone of voice falls at the end of each sentence to accentuate their importance and they leave lots of pauses.

And most people when faced with someone who sounds ever so important will put you through without hesitation. Try it, it's fun as well.

"Hello, Paul Archer here, CEO Archer Training. Mike Brown please."

Said in the right way will have many gatekeepers reaching for the transfer button.

Know your prospect

Gatekeepers have been asked by their boss to only put through important calls, so we should help them to appreciate how important our call is.

Don't sell to the Gate-opener; it's a waste of time and effort. It also devalues the message you have. If it's sufficiently easy for the Gate-opener to make a decision on it, why do you need to speak to anyone else?

Some possible phrases:

"Hi, is Martin there right now?". This infers that you know each other well.

"Could you put me through to Martin please, Martin Smith". This infers that you already know each other well. This begins to make the decision to say "no" difficult.

If asked who you are: "Sure, it's Lynn here, Lynn Smith". Again, by emphasising the first name it infers that you already know each other well.

If asked what your call is about: "Yes, of course; it's in connection with the Association's recent recommendation".

Even better, if a letter has been sent in advance: "Yes, of course, Martin's expecting my call today; it's in connection with the Associations' recent recommendation".

You may all the same be asked: "Can you tell me and I'll pass it on…". Keep focused on the goal and continue to make the decision to say "no" difficult …. "I could do, but in all honesty there are so many potential issues that in order to provide [organisation] with the correct and appropriate information relevant to the recommendations I really could do with chatting with Martin directly for a couple of ticks. Thank you."

The 7am call

This is a very useful tip that you can use for a number of situations in prospecting. It's best left for keeping in touch with prospects who you've qualified, but don't have an immediate need. Kind of the "keep us informed" brigade. But of course you could use it with existing clients as a way of keeping in touch.

The premise is that making a call to their mobile at around 7am'ish will not get through but you leave a voice mail message. The message is up to you but make sure you include some benefit to them.

So how does the person react when they hear the message? It'll probably be their first voice mail of the day so they'll most likely listen to it going to work. This means your message gets their maximum attention.

The early time might impress them and think you're an early bird. Or they'll think you're a workaholic. Either way it doesn't matter – the intention was to get remembered, and you've achieved that.

Call outside of "meeting hours".

The biggest reason that people aren't at their desk, is that they're in meetings and this is normally correct as busy buyers are up to their necks in meetings.

Try avoiding 10 to 12pm and 2 to 4pm.

Screech in from high

Here's a handy idea if you're having trouble getting through to a new client or prospect on the telephone.

Watching the Battle of Britain on the TV for the hundredth time at the weekend, I was impressed with the tactics that the Spitfire fighter aircraft used in their battle against the enemy planes.

The most successful were the fighters who had height on their side, and could screech from high altitude on top of the enemy. It worked in the Battle of Britain. Great film.

Here's a little tip to come in from high with any potential gatekeeper.

Phone the head person in the company, say it's Dawn Somers the CEO. You'll get through to her Personal Assistant probably. Ask to speak with the person who deals with whatever you sell. Be as pleasant as possible and the PA will probably say to speak with Brian or Bob or Marcia, as she knows pretty much everyone in the company. You might be lucky and get to speak with the MD, but it's unlikely.

Next you phone your target prospect, and get through to their PA. Now you use the genuine reason that Dawn Somer's PA asked me to get in touch with you, I'm Paul Archer from xyz.

It works because you're coming in from a respected high position, just like my Spitfires from the sky above.

Other gatekeeper ideas

If you've rung before and you've been told, "Martin is away in Wales" this is a great opportunity to start off the call by saying "Hi, it's Lynn here. Is Martin back from Wales yet or do I need to catch him tomorrow?" It's sending a clear message that you not only know each other, but you know each other sufficiently well for you to know his diary.

Most companies operate a direct dial facility for their staff. Whenever possible, ask the switchboard for the direct dial number of the person you want. Indeed, it is not infrequent that this information can be found on the organisation's web site.

You can even call through to the wrong extension, and with a tone of surprise in your voice say "…Oh, sorry – I was trying to get through to Martin Jones. You can't put me through from your extension can you? Thanks."

Vocal Cosmetics

Verbal tics

"Uh", "hurs", "right", "yea" or other verbal tics can be really bothersome. Here's a simple way to see if you have them or not. Next time you're chatting to friends, casually place your cupped hands over your ears. Keep talking naturally and you'll soon see if you use them more than you should.

The trick is to train yourself to pause instead, or take a breath. Try and learn to live with the odd second or two of silence.

Breathe like a singer

This will allow you to use your voice to maximum effect with little extra effort. Most people breathe from the chest and you can see this by watching someone's shoulders go up and down as they breathe. Now singers breathe from the diaphragm which is pretty much just behind your tummy and this gives you much more air from the same amount of effort.

You probably normally breathe from your chest (noticeable by your rib cage moving up and down), but you can also breathe from your diaphragm (evident by your stomach moving in and out). Put your hand on your stomach and breathe deeply so that your hand moves in and out.

This is abdominal breathing and it allows you to access the lower/richer end of your voice range. If you use abdominal breathing while speaking, you can also take in more air and thus talk for longer without pausing (useful for presentations).

Try it. See if you can breathe from your diaphragm – it'll make it much easier to talk.

Are you too quick?

Everyone in this world speaks at a different speed. Some people can speak mega quick and seem to understand other fast talkers as well. But unfortunately most of us can't keep up with the Speedy Gonzalezes and struggle to understand. Speaking at about 2½ to 3½ words a second is about right.

Test your speed by saying for me:

"Are you copper bottoming 'em my man?

No, I'm aluminiuming 'em ma'am"

It should take just under 5 seconds to read it without stumbling over the big word at the end. Any faster and you need to slow down when on the phone.

And if you took too long, I think my aluminiuming got the better of you.

Remember too fast and you will come over as a pushy salesperson, too slow and they might think about you being bottom of the class.

Stretch your vocal range

How big is yours?

I mean your vocal range. Can you move your voice from low to high with little difficulty? If you can, it makes your voice more interesting to listen to, easier to match your customer's voice and it can make the job more fun.

Why all the fuss? If you have a narrow vocal range, in other words, you sound monotonous, then your customers will soon delete your voice. Sounds painful but people can only concentrate on about 7 things hitting their senses before they delete you out.

It's like sitting on the fast train and having that da dum, da dum or watching a clock tick. Before you know it you're asleep.

Slightly over the top but my point is made.

Here's a couple of things you can do to exercise your vocal range to expand it.

Read out loud children's books, but it's not so easy if you don't have children.

Another idea is to count from one to ten going from low pitch to high and then back down again. You can do this out loud only I'm afraid so make sure you have your friends with you.

Did you know that in a phone conversation, your attitude is conveyed within your voice almost 30 times more than when you're face to face with someone.

12 vocal cosmetic tips

Eliminate verbal viruses

Train yourself to pause or a breath whenever you catch yourself saying your favourite non-word. You can actually pause for up to 3 or 4 seconds to gather your thoughts.

Enlist the help of a friend of colleague. Tell them which word(s) you are trying to avoid and ask them to let you know whenever they hear those words slip into your speech.

Never cradle the receiver

When you cradle the receiver between your ear and shoulder it gives your voice a muffled "I'm calling for the ransom money" sound. Using a headset will prevent this problem and help keep you out of the chiropractor's office with neck strain.

Avoid using the speaker phone

No one sounds their best on the speaker phone. It makes you sound as if you are calling from the bathroom and it's just plain rude because the caller doesn't know who else may be in the room listening.

Chair and workstation

Believe it or not, the quality of your desk chair and your work station can affect the sound of your voice. You won't sound your best if you are hunched over your keyboard or leaning way back in your chair. Sit up straight for good breath support and position your computer monitor at eye level so your chin doesn't have to tilt up or down.

Stay hydrated

Drinking plenty of water is not only good for your overall well-being, it's good for the health of your voice. A thin layer of mucus covers the respiratory tract and this mucus should be thin and runny for the vocal folds to stay well lubricated. Drinking 8-10 glasses of water daily will help.

Avoid these phlegm monsters

Certain foods can really gunk up your voice. On important speaking days avoid dairy; fried, oily or fatty foods; and mayonnaise.

Avoid these vocal dehydrators

The following foods are dehydrating and can affect the natural lubrication of the vocal folds:

- Caffeinated beverages: coffee, tea, colas
- Chocolate
- Mints, mint tea
- Air conditioning and heating. Use a humidifier in the winter

Visualise your customer

Your telephone voice will sound warmer and more personable if you visualise the person you are speaking to.

Paint a clear mental picture of the person on the other end of the phone, even if you have never met them face-to-face.

Don't stare off into space when you speak on the phone. Keep your eyes focused as if making eye contact.

Keep a photo of a loved one by the phone and make eye contact with the photo to help keep a "blank stare" out of your voice.

Use livelier body language

Animating your body language will really add energy and enthusiasm to your voice. Use the same body language as if you were face to face with your listener.

Imagine that the person on the other end of the phone is sitting on the other side of your desk and lean toward them as if to share a confidence.

Speak with your hands

Smile when you speak and use a mirror to make sure the expression on your face is a pleasant one.

- Sit up straight
- Stand periodically to boost your vocal energy level
- Project your voice

Voice too soft?

If people complain that you speak too softly over the phone:

- Check your equipment. Is your phone working properly? Does your headset need new batteries? Are you speaking with the microphone close enough to your mouth?
- Change your imagined proximity to the listener. Speak as if they are several feet away, not inches away from your mouth
- Use your hands while you speak. It adds energy to your voice

People first, then paperwork

Keep paperwork out of your visual field to avoid being distracted.

Never multi-task while speaking on the phone. Callers can tell if you are checking your email, filing your nails or washing your dishes while you speak.

Don't do anything while speaking on the phone that you wouldn't do if you were face-to-face with the caller.

Openers

Warm up your prospect

A short while ago my Independent Adviser phoned me and said Happy Birthday Paul. I was taken aback although this is one of the first tricks they teach you at life assurance selling school. You give your date of birth as part of the process, so good advisers note your birthday and send you a card or phone you up on your birthday.

But Charlie still made me smile that morning.

A good tip for you is to keep an eye on movers and shakers, promotions and such in your industry and then phone these people to congratulate them. Lots of salespeople think this is too corny so don't do it – more for us to contact then.

Google does a great service that sends you links about companies that you are prospecting. I set this up with Google noting all my clients and prospects and I got an email saying that someone had left for an important position with another company. I had met this person briefly so I sent them a card and followed this up with a phone call congratulating him on his new position and mentioning what I do.

Everyone likes to be congratulated or praised or thanked – it's one of life's certainties, so next time you're on the phone to a prospect, warm them up with some carefully chosen congratulations or warm thoughts.

Is it convenient to talk?

Its courtesy, it's a cold call Code of Conduct that firms train to their salespeople, it's something ingrained in our core.

But it can lead to an early dismissal.

Instead re-word it like so:

"Hi Bob, if I've caught you at a good time, I'd like to…."

Questions are the answer

As salespeople, especially salespeople who use the phone regularly, we just so know that we need to ask questions. And the sooner we get to ask a question the better as it stops us talking, digging holes, and turns the attention back to the prospect.

But too many salespeople go into a one way tirade of the benefits they can give to the prospect and give them little chance to respond.

So the best tip I can offer is to ask a question almost in your first breath.

"Hello Bob, we specialise in … so to determine if this might be valuable for you I'd like to learn more about your challenges…."

So remember…questions are the answer.

The 90 second opener

Now that you're through to your customer, you want to get things moving along and take control.

And no you don't want to start talking about the weather or the football game or the state of the nation. Unless they want you to.

Building rapport on the telephone is a little more deeper than that and we'll look at this later.

No, you want to do two processes in 90 seconds – the Agenda Statement and the Credibility Statement.

Agenda statements

During your pre-call planning you would have checked the hook that you left from your last call, in other words the compelling reason to phone them. Use this in the agenda unless it's a new call, where you'll want to arouse their curiosity with the reason for your call.

These should be used for every call however informal. Alpha type clients love them particularly and the best structure is the POINT plan.

1. Purpose of call
2. Outline what you'll cover
3. Input – is there anything they'd like to cover – only if this is a follow on call
4. Transition – onto the meeting itself

Agenda statements are verbal agendas, obviously.

"Hello Bob, if it's convenient to talk right now I'd like to talk to you about some exciting new things we're doing here at ABC to help IFAs bring in more revenue. I'll need about 7 minutes of your time, if that's OK. Firstly I'd like to tell you about me."

Or

"Hi Jane, it's Nigel here from ABC, how are you today?

That's great. I'm calling you today because I promised I'd get back to you with some testimonials from other IFAs about our service. We'll need 8 minutes to go over these and I would hope at the end of the call, you'll become a big fan of ours. Is there anything else you would like this call to cover?

OK, let's have a look at an email I received from…"

Credibility statement

Used when you're on the phone to a new broker and you do need to practise this big time. 4 steps:

1. Your company and you. Tell them something about your company and you.
2. Typical customers that you help.
3. A short success story.
4. Transition. "So that's me…how about you?"

Drafting your credibility statement

Take a blank piece of paper and write down 8-10 key facts about your firm. Things like:

- When it was founded
- What the company specialises in
- Awards
- Number of employees, buyers, assets, etc.

Now write down 4-5 key facts about you. Things like:

- How long you've been with the company
- How long you've been in the industry
- Why you like your company
- Any qualifications/licences you may have

Next think about who your typical buyers are. You can call them by name, industry, or need.

Success Story

It's important to have several success stories at the ready so you can interchange them to best fit the buyer you are speaking to. Aim for half a dozen.

- Buyer:
- Issue:
- Resolution:
- Benefit: (Pound'ise it if possible)

Now write out your complete credibility statement and practise it 4 times.

Signposting

Keep your customer posted

My 8 year old daughter was loading two new computer games on her laptop, which she'd borrowed from her brother: Zoo Tycoon and Frankie Secret Agent. She was so excited.

Frankie Secret Agent seemed to load OK and Bethan was thrilled to get the game started so she clicked on the start button. However, the screen went blank and a small graphic in the middle of the screen stated simply that the game was loading.

And still loading 5 minutes later. And the same 5 minutes after that.

"How long will this take Daddy?"

"I've no idea Bethy; have some patience and leave it be."

Words of wisdom from Daddy, who was a little busy, as always.

45 minutes later she returned and the same message was on the screen.

"I'm really upset with this Daddy what should I do?"

"Eject it and load Zoo Tycoon if you want." So she did, but this time the experience was completely different.

This time the message came up saying loading but it had a graphic showing where the loading was in the great scheme of loading. It also mentioned what was being added during the process, for example "Now loading the animals, now the zoo keepers, here come the buildings..."

It was keeping Bethan informed and she loved it. It kept her attention and patience to see it to the end even though the loading sequence took almost 10 minutes – 10 minutes seems like a lifetime to an 8 year old.

When in the middle of a coaching session, a sales meeting or a business presentation, we need to remember that customers and coachees need to know where they are in the process – that way we keep their attention and interest so use signposting techniques. The oldest adage is to "tell 'em what you're going to cover, then tell them as you approach each element of you process and then tell 'em what you covered at the end as a summary".

Don't keep them in the dark otherwise they'll lose interest like my daughter and her laptop.

Isn't it amazing what 8 year olds enjoy nowadays with Xbox Live, laptops, MSN and computer games – when I was 8, I was lucky to get to watch black and white TV, play Knock

Down Ginger with my mates, fall about laughing so hard that my stomach hurt, reach into a muddy gutter for a penny…and that was after I came up from the coal mine.

Signpost at the beginning of the call

This month I've been doing tons of coaching with call centre people who take calls from the public about their insurance policies.

Some of the callers are really good and some not so, naturally. They all vary in their skills. But one thing that the good ones all do is signpost the beginning of the call.

The importance of signposting whether you are phoning out on a sales call or taking incoming calls, hit me when I got to listen to one call handled by a particularly sound call handler. The customer had experienced a major calamity. A water pipe had burst and completely flooded her front room. Now this lady carefully explained that she had never before claimed on her insurance and had no idea what to expect.

She was very apprehensive.

So immediately my call handling friend began to signpost her to relax her and to ensure she knew what was going to happen next on the phone.

The lady was told that the call would probably last about 8 minutes, and they could both complete the claim form over the telephone with little fuss. There was no need for paper, as my friend would complete the form on the computer so there would be quite a few questions. Was she sitting comfortably?

Sometimes we assume the customer knows exactly what will happen on the call because we've dealt with hundreds if not thousands. But this was the customer's first call and the signposting helped relax her and sort out her claim.

Never assume.

Signposting through silences

A good friend of mine has a terrific voice, so good in fact that we call him Golden Tonsils. He often gets work from TV companies and theatre companies to do voice over work or he gets to narrate plays.

Now his work is directly connected to handling people on the telephone.

Let me explain further.

When you're talking face to face with someone, we can cope with the odd silent moment. It's obvious when someone looks away to think about what we've just been talking about, or looks down to complete a section on a form, or just takes notes as we talk.

On the phone, however, silent moments, are just …silent and devoid of all human interaction.

Good phone handlers use the signposting technique to explain why the silent moment has occurred or use it to pre-warn when a silent moment will happen during the call.

"It may go quiet for a little bit as I need to complete the details section of the page, I won't keep you too long"

In fact good call handlers almost narrate the phone call as it occurs, letting the customer know exactly what's happening at each step of the way.

Just like my friend with the golden tonsils.

27 Rapport Building Tips

1. Be adaptable

Agents should be able to adapt their approach – there is no reason to think that all customers should be approached using the same style. Use personal experience to build rapport so that the caller feels you are putting yourself in their shoes.

2. Pace and lead

This technique is extremely useful when someone is in an over-excited state. Start by showing urgency, confidence and concern in your speech patterns and manner to match and reassure them.

Then gradually begin to calm and slow up your speech patterns. As long as the customer feels things are happening and that you're in rapport, they will follow you down and become calmer in response.

3. Allow them to 'get it all out'

When the customer is angry, allow them to vent without interruption. Use this time to figure out what you can do to fix their issue.

4. Repeat back

Repeat sentences or important details back to the customer, saying "Okay, just to recap…"

This reassures them that you are paying attention.

5. Be aware of your intonation

Go up at the end of the sentence for questions, go down at the end for command (discourage further debate).

6. Get their name first

Ask for the customer's name first, rather than reference number, address, etc.

It is easy to get the details we need after we have their name. This makes the customer feel like an individual and agents feel as if they are speaking with a person, not a caller.

7. Make their problem your problem

Take ownership of the enquiry, especially if it is a complaint. Have a one-to-one relationship with your customer so that they have a point of contact that they can come back to.

8. See it from the customer's perspective

Encourage agents to imagine themselves in the customer's shoes. Or, if they are struggling to display empathy, ask them to imagine the customer as a close friend or family member.

9. Share their priorities

Every customer, particularly in an emergency situation, will have a list of priorities. Making them also your priorities and addressing them in the right order (mirroring them) will reassure them that you know what they want and are taking care of them.

10. Remember the value of an apology

For those who deal with complaints all the time – a simple, genuine apology at the appropriate time can defuse a difficult customer and break down the barriers to allow space to build rapport.

11. You don't have to have 'things in common'

Some agents may worry that they do not have anything in common with their customers and will therefore be unable to build rapport. But this doesn't have to be the case.

Our contact centre is based on a particular sport – the best agents with the best customer service skills don't always share our customers' love of the sport.

12. Don't rush

Sometimes agents can identify an issue they have seen regularly and then rush to rectify the problem quickly. But it's always best to focus on building rapport first.

13. Smile

Always start the call with a smile – the customer will notice this in your voice.

14. Take a personal interest

You can build rapport by showing a personal interest in the customer. For example, if a customer says they have been in hospital, ask them how the recovery is going.

If you were speaking to somebody face-to-face and they told you that they had just come out of hospital, you would normally check how they are.

15. Know what you're selling

Know your product well enough to know your customer – this is where rapport begins.

16. Really listen

Be a good a listener and try to repeat what the customer says to assure them that you are listening.

17. Be respectful

Make sure you talk to the customer with respect and in common language. Never talk down to them.

18. Start off with something positive

If the customer has spent some time explaining a frustrating problem to you, then beginning your response with a short, direct statement of intent can gain the customer's confidence.

Something like "Okay, we can fix this…" or "Right, let's get this problem sorted for you…" will reassure the customer that you are taking ownership of the problem.

19. Keep focused

Stay one hundred percent focused on the customer and don't let colleagues or other things in the office distract you.

If the customer doesn't have your full attention, they will always pick up on it.

20. Not all customers want to chat

Remember that angry customers don't want to build rapport – they just want to tell you what the problem is and for you to fix it.

21. Avoid assumptions

Don't make assumptions about what the customer is telling you – actively listen!

22. End on a high

Always ask the customer if there is anything else you can do for them before you end the call. This shows that your priority is giving good service, not just getting the call over with.

23. Be flexible with formality

We address our customers in the way that they introduce themselves. The screen may show them as Christopher Jones, but if the customer calls himself Chris, we will address them in the same way.

Some customers prefer to keep things more formal and may introduce themselves as Mr Jones. It depends on the business.

24. Smile through the complaints

You need to always smile, even when the customer is complaining. They don't want to hear that the agent is having a bad day – they want to know that you will be able to solve the issue and then in turn make the customer smile.

25. Don't linger on the tough calls

Leave the last call behind and start afresh every time. Every customer is different.

26. Beware of inappropriate jokes

Everyone must be careful with humour. Sometimes there is too high a risk of a jokey comment being misunderstood, just like sarcasm in emails.

27. Don't leave them waiting

Be careful when putting people on hold or transferring calls – this can damage rapport as wait times always seem longer when you are lingering in dead space.

Listening on the Phone

What's the worst sin of a telephone salesperson?

It was a really important sales training event involving all sorts of video technology so I was planning and practising the gadgets on the boardroom table. Cameras were wired up to DVD recorders, players were running pre-recorded DVDs and the projector was presenting the whole scene on the wall. There were cables strewn everywhere but it seemed to be working. I thought I'd cracked it.

Until the phone rang.

It was my long lost Uncle Ivan who can never take a hint about convenient times to call or that someone else might be a tad busy. Ivan was an Oil Super Tanker Captain for BP throughout his career and was used to spending long voyages of 6 to 7 months with only a handful of people at any time. It's not that he can talk for England but he's very clever at asking questions to get you talking and being provocative to encourage conversation. All those years with only a small bunch of shipmates to keep him company.

So what did I do? I carried on listening in one ear and finishing off my complex wiring strategy for the video equipment.

Did I listen? A bit, but not enough to strike up anything meaningful with my Uncle Ivan and after the call, I felt really guilty as I'd spurned the chance of rekindling our relationship.

And I'd committed the cardinal sin of all telephone salespeople. The disease that causes more telesales people to not listen to their customers that anything else: Multitasking.

It has to be the biggest distraction. Taking a call and doing something else whilst they're talking. We know full well that clicking on emails won't affect the call or typing a web address won't cause concern with the customer but this multitasking does stop us from effectively listening to the customer.

Beware of multitasking – we're all guilty of it from time to time and it's normally always recognised by customers. When someone is typing on their keyboard and listening to me, I can hear them tapping away and it annoys me.

And my Uncle Ivan. I phoned him back the next day and he's popping up for Sunday Dinner next month. My wife can hardly wait!

A listening MOT

Look at the following questions. How do these apply to you and the way you listen? Please answer honestly. Ask yourself...

1. Are you doing something else while the customer is talking? Yes/No

2. Are you thinking about the next call, going out that evening, what you will be eating for dinner? Yes/No

3. During your conversation with a customer, do you wait for a pause, so you can say something? Yes/No

4. How difficult is it for you to stay quiet - do you say something without thinking first? Yes/No

5. Are you faking your listening to the customer, just so you can get in your comments? Yes/No

6. Do you practise selective listening? Do you only hear the things you want to hear? Yes/No

7. Are you unaware of the message being sent by other means than just the client's words (e.g., language, key phrases, mood, vocal intonation)? Yes/No

8. Do you allow background noise or your environment to hinder your ability to listen? Yes/No

Maybe I've insulted you with some of these questions but this was not my intention. I just wanted you to be aware of how difficult listening can be and how easy we can slip into bad habits.

Self awareness is the first step to improvement.

Your own volume control

Listening on the telephone in fact listening in general, has to be one of the hardest things to do continuously. Yes we can all listen for five minute bursts but to do it all day every day, just has to be hard graft.

So next time you feel your listening ability has taken an early bath, imagine your very own personal volume control.

Now your volume control has 3 levels – 1, 2 and 3.

Most of the time it's on level 1 which is selfish listening and there's nothing wrong with this. Only the other day I was on a business trip to a strange airport and I was operating on level 1 listening. I was looking out for signs and noises that would help me on my journey. I wasn't interested in anyone else just myself and my next steps.

But in selling or dealing with people on the phone, we mustn't focus on just ourselves. We need to get into their shoes and that's level 2 on your volume control.

Turn up the volume and start to think of the world in their shoes. How do they see things, have empathy for their situation, understand their world?

Have you spoken to a friend recently that has just returned from a holiday abroad to the same place as you've been? Did you find yourself comparing their experience with yours? I bet you did. I do, until I kick myself back into level 2 listening.

Finally there's volume level 3. Rarely do we cross into this level. Here we begin to hear and see things around our customer that are not obvious. We develop a kind of sixth sense so we can hear what's not being said as well as what's being said.

They call it intuition. Trust it, as it won't let you down.

So next time you're on the telephone and you're struggling to listen, think of your imaginary volume control.

Reflective statements

These are very handy little devices that show the customer that you're listening and help to build empathy.

These are used to reflect emotion; they can act as a valuable tool in building rapport. If someone is perhaps angry, or very excited, or anxious – this emotion is probably going to get in the way of our discussion. Until we have in some way handled this emotion, we may not get their full concentration on what we need to find out.

- "I can understand how that could be frustrating"
- "I can see how that would be upsetting"
- "You seem annoyed about something"

It gives the person the chance to vent their feelings and emotion. Make the statement and pause for 1½ seconds for a response. Learn to be comfortable with a little bit of silence before you have to signpost your way through it.

Verbal nods

Imagine having a conversation with a good friend in a coffee shop and she gets to the best bit. What do you do? Yes you lean forward, give eye contact, nod your head, match expressions.

Yes, you are showing good non verbal listening skills, often called active listening.

The disadvantage of the telephone is we don't have body language to help us listen, or show that we're listening. Classics such as nodding, eye contact, eye brow movement all help to show we're listening.

But without sight we have to go totally verbal.

- "Uh hur"
- "I see"
- "Keep going"
- "That's interesting"
- "Oh dear"

The list goes on and each one tells the customer that you're listening to them.

Care though you don't use the same one as this will soon become what's known as a "verbal tic".

Beware the verbal tic.

Eliminating distractions

One of my first sales jobs was working as a financial adviser for a busy estate agent in a major city. My desk was right by a large picture window opening up to Guildford High Street. On a Saturday or a busy lunchtime, hundreds of people would walk by, some would stare in at me. Cars and trucks would drive by and there would always be some movement going on outside.

And meanwhile I had to use the phone to speak with customers.

I also recall the very next day being told in the morning that the company I worked for was up for sale. Suddenly the external distraction of the window didn't matter, as my head was full of internal distractions this time to prevent me from listening to my customer.

It's so difficult selling on the phone when the world is full of distractions.

External distractions

I'm always amazed when I'm coaching people who use the phone all the time, how many distractions there are that can prevent you from listening 100% to the customer. There's always people coming up asking if you want a cup of tea, people wandering around, some people making lots of noise. A general buzz.

A useful exercise is to make a list of all the external things that can cause you distraction and then make some decision about what you can do about them, so as to minimise their effect. Here are a few examples:

- Distractions on desk
- Distractions on screen
- Noise in the office
- Colleagues interrupting
- Watching colleagues

Internal distractions

Equally annoying are the internal distractions that dominate our thoughts. The fact is we speak at about 150 words per minute, but think at 750 words a minute. So you can see why our head is always so full of words and self talk.

So how do we fill the gap? Here's some examples of internal distractions:

- Daydreaming – half listening though mind wandering off
- Filtering - hearing what you want to hear
- Making assumptions – you know what they mean already
- Rehearsing – thinking about what you are going to say next
- Placating – right...yes...I know...absolutely...you are being nice and agree with everything

Easier said than done, but the key here is to understand your internal distractions – identify them and then make a decision to fix them.

Summarising to listen

Because using the telephone eliminates the body language side of communication we have to accentuate certain other communication skills to make up for this.

One of these is the art of summarising.

Observation of excellent call handlers and telephone salespeople shows that not only do they summarise what's been agreed at the end of the call, which many of us do, but they regularly summarise throughout the call.

Summarising throughout the call can:

- Show the customer you have listened
- Allow you to keep control of the call
- Helps you direct and signpost the call
- Shows empathy with the customer

- Helps to interrupt long-winded customers

So how do we summarise? That's like saying how do you eat Cornflakes for breakfast? It's easy…you pour in the cornflakes and then follow up with the milk.

Likewise summarising is not difficult…you start one with a phrase such as:

- "Let me see if I've followed you so far…."
- "OK, let me recap…."
- "Let me check…"
- "Let me check I've got everything…."
- "What you're saying is…"
- "Can I just go over your main issues…."
- "Can I stop you and make sure I'm with you…"

Then you summarise and ask the customer if I missed anything.

Remember to summarise a little bit more during the call and not just at the end.

Questioning on the Phone

The fallacy of open questions

Open questions versus closed questions. This battle has been fought for years and no one is the clear winner. However a good open question does lend itself to a fuller answer from your customer. But the trick is to know how to follow up.

Anyway here's a reminder of the six open questions from Rudyard Kipling's famous poems:

"I keep six honest serving men

(They taught me all I knew);

Their names are What and Why and When

And How and Where and Who"

The dangerous one here is "why?" It's proven to be antagonistic and annoying to the receiver. When faced with the "why" question, many customers will raise their defences as they feel as though they are being attacked.

Interesting.

The other problem with questions is shown by the rest of Kipling's poem:

"I know a person small -

She keeps ten million serving men,

Who get no rest at all!

She sends 'em abroad on her own affairs,

From the second she opens her eyes -

One million Hows, Two million Wheres,

And seven Million Whys!"

Take care we don't turn into a military interrogator.

Softening your questions - beware the rising tone?

"It's called early teenage talk".

That was the response from a teenage expert after I asked about the irritating habit I've noticed my teenage son using when talking to his friends. "It's called teenage talk".

So what is this annoying habit that causes this grumpy old man to moan about?

It's the constant rising tonality of every sentence that my son uses. His sentences start normal and then his voice rises at the end of the phrase or sentence. This continues for hours. Have you noticed it from people?

Now it's not going to harm anyone and I should move on to worry about more important things but it actually is important in sales. More than people think.

We all know that communication is more than just the words chosen. Plenty of research carried out over the last 30 years shows that face to face communication consists of three parts – the words, the way you say them and the body language that's used to launch the words. The tone of the voice has a remarkable influence on the meaning, more that we think.

Straightforward really. A flat tone tells you that the sentence is just a statement. A falling tone indicates a command and a rising sentence says there is a question here.

Try it now. Say something like, "It's time to go to bed". Say it with a flat, falling and then a rising tone and listen to the impact. It really works doesn't it?

Now this little gem has a couple of practical sales uses. I like practical don't you?

Firstly when asking a question to find out your customer's needs and pains, make the questioning more palatable for them by raising your tone a little. This makes the question you ask much more pleasing to the ear and you'll never be accused of interrogating your customer.

Secondly, when you want your customer to do something, drop your tone a little but only just a little. "So Bob, you're happy to go ahead with the paperwork then?" It's constructed as a question but the customer will accept it as a command. A little hypnotic maybe but your customer will do as you wish.

Now why do teenagers talk with rising tones on every sentence? I've no idea. It's probably something to do with wanting a reaction to everything they say and so raising the tone in your sentence makes it sound like a question.

Or it's just one of those things my teenage son does to irritate a grumpy old man like me!

Pre-Conditioning

Gosh that's a terrible title don't you think? Pre-conditioning…sounds like something you do in the shower!

But it can be really useful when selling on the telephone especially when asking questions. The theory works like this. Humans like to be told what's coming up next, in other words to be pre-conditioned, so when it happens it's not so much of a shock.

Let me give you an example. Many moons ago when I worked in estate agency, we had a property that refused to sell. Admittedly it was a little run down, in need of some urgent tender loving care, but a decent house for the price. But it refused to shift and we couldn't realise why.

Until we had some feedback from a buyer who said that the roads on the way in were awful and just put them off before they even got to the house. So when they arrived at the home they were pre-conditioned to not like it.

So the next applicant who was interested to have a look, was swiftly put in the manager's BMW and driven to the house. Admittedly it was the long way there but the journey we chose was much more amenable and pleasant and put the applicant in the best frame of mind to view the house.

And it worked too!

Another practical tip is to use pre-conditions in your language when presenting to customers. I like to use the phrase "I've left the best to last"…and "here it is" or "and here's the best news…"

You see, you're pre-conditioning the next part of your statement and this is a really useful technique when asking questions that are a little tough.

- "Mr Brown, would you be able to tell me please…."
- "I hope you're OK for me to ask…"
- "May I ask…."
- "I'd be curious to know…."
- "I'd be very interested to know…"
- "Tell me…"

The last point to mention about pre-conditioning is a trap I often hear salespeople falling into.

Don't pre-condition negatively for example,

- "I'm sorry to ask this…."
- "We have to talk about the cost now I'm afraid"
- "I hope you don't mind me asking but…"

You see you're simply negatively pre-conditioning them with your language.

Types of questions

Function	Probe	Definition	Characteristics	Use to
Getting the customer to open up	Open-end probes	Questions or requests that get wide-ranging response on a broad subject	Usually begin with – *what, how, tell me.*	Open up silent customers.
	Probe questions	Designed to probe deeper on an issue	Focus on a subject. "That's interesting what you said about..."	Get more information on a specific subject.
	Hypothetical questions	Places customer in unfamiliar position to explore alternatives. "If you were ill right now, what effect would this have on your family?"	Use words "imagine" or "what if..."	Encourage customer to explore pains.
Getting the customer to keep on talking	Pauses	Short silences that let the customer mull over and respond to what he's heard	Relax pace so the customer doesn't feel pressured. Lets you collect thoughts and plan.	Encourage silent customers to respond.
	Verbal and Non-Verbal Nods	Short statements that encourage customer to keep talking. Plus non verbal such as nodding, eye brow moving	Maintain good rapport. Usually produce additional information.	Encourage customer to say more.
Making sure you understand	Closed-end questions	Questions worded to produce short, precise answers	Excellent for getting final commitment and gathering details.	Focus on specifics and control roaming. Yes tags work well here.
	Summary statements	Statements that summarise information obtained from customer	Focus on facts, not emotions. Help customer clarify own thinking by hearing it summed up by you.	Gratify customer's esteem by showing you're listening. Focus on relevant facts. Separate wheat from chaff.

6 Cute questioning tips

Playback

This simple little idea is very useful to encourage your customer to talk more on an issue they've just brought up.

Simply repeat back what they just said with a slight rise in your tone to make it a question.

"Oh"

This little word "oh" is so powerful. Use it with your customers and remember to lift your tone a little as well. And it's guaranteed to show your interest in what the customer is saying and will get them telling some more.

"Really"

Similar to the "oh" and again this will get your customer saying more on the subject they're talking about.

Pause

Telephone salespeople are often very uncomfortable with silence and will do anything they can to hide it, often just talking or waffling through.

The trick is to get yourself comfortable with 1 to 2 seconds of silence. On the phone this can feel like a lifetime but if your customer has something else to say, the pause will encourage them to say it.

Machine gunning

You hear this style of questions from radio and TV interviewers who aren't very good at their trade. They rattle off 3 or 4 questions all at once and it's called machine gunning. The reason is that the first question they don't like, so they re-phrase it and ask it differently and then they ask something else that came into their mind.

All it does is confuse the customer.

Bite your lip the next time you ask a series of questions. Bite your lip after the first one, if it's a dumb question, just accept it and ask a better one next time.

How do you feel?

The next time your customer goes quiet and you are itching to fill in the gap, ask the question "How do you feel so far?", or "How does that sound to you?"

Ask about their buying process

I was recently at a meeting with a potential client and we arrived at the proposal stage. Now proposals are a long winded affair and can take a long time to produce, proof read and send on.

So I asked my client "Do you want detail or top line?"

Thankfully he only wanted top line!

But the point is to ask your customer how they want to be sold to, handled or dealt with. This tip is useful both when selling to individuals or businesses and it involves asking questions to find out how they buy.

- "How did you choose your current supplier?"

- "What type of budget have you set aside for this?"

- "If we went ahead with this, who else would be involved?"

- "How's the best way for me to show you the benefits of this?"

Try asking a few questions around their preferred process and it just might shave a little time from your sales process.

Fact finding over the phone

Improve your knowledge

All competent salespeople know their products – the features and benefits, the problems they solve and good salespeople know all the objections that are thrown at them and can overcome them all.

This knowledge is a mandatory need.

No, I mean knowledge in two other areas – your industry and your client's business. You need to be the expert on your industry, current trends, global issues. A sales friend of mine is particularly good at predicting industry changes and is known as a futurist. Clients ask him to share this knowledge with staff as well as themselves.

Do you read the right publications, are you Googling the industry and the main players who might be your client's competition? Are you ahead of the game when it comes to changes and events and product changes? Are you abreast of taxation and government policy towards your industry? To become a trusted adviser you must be totally focused in this area.

Knowledge of your client is just as important. Your early inroads will be fact finding, you'll have various contacts within the client's company who can give you inside information, ask lots of questions and really get to understand your client's company. The most important knowledge to have of your client are their problems, pains, issues and challenges. What keeps them up at night? What's the number one focus this year? What one problem do you really need solving to move forward on your targets?

Become a problem solver

You already know your industry problems and also your client's problems. The next skill is to be able to creatively solve these for them, ideally using your products or services or a combination of each. But a true trusted adviser may give expertise to solve problems with their product being involved because they know that the loyalty the client has, will fill their order book.

Sometimes your client may not even appreciate they have these problems that you know about or how they can be solved. Your questions will reveal them and allow you to solve them.

For example, an IFA consultant friend of mine was telling me a story of an IFA he was keen to do business with. The questions my friend asked were designed to find out more about the IFA's issues and problems and they revealed that he had a morbid fear of presenting in public. Now for this IFA to admit this there had to be incredible rapport and trust between the two of them.

The business the IFA wanted to enter into was key man insurance and this involves presenting to boards and groups of influencers within companies. So to solve the problem my IFA consultant friend said he'd do all the stand up presenting for him as he was particularly skilled in this area. Worked a treat.

The IFA was successful in this market area and the consultant reaped the benefits with some large cases going his way. My friend also arranged some training for the IFA to boost his confidence when speaking in public and this further cemented the relationship they had.

Many years ago, as an IFA Training Consultant for a life office, I was working with one of our IFA consultants who wanted to penetrate business with a new IFA on his panel. His consultative questioning revealed that the IFA was looking to expand in business and was struggling to keep up with the back office side of things and was struggling to recruit the right people. We organised some recruitment training and an assessment day for the IFA, and as a result, he was able to recruit some excellent support staff who we then helped train to become paraplanners.

And as a result this IFA became a huge supporter of the life office.

The skills to solve problems

Our job as salespeople is to help the customer realise the pain that they are in with their current situation and to get them ready to receive favourably our solution to take away this pain.

Now pushy salespeople tell customers this and they suggest products to make it better. They then overcome every objection and force a sale.

Consultancy salespeople build a long term relationship with customers, ask lots of questions to help the customer realise their needs and pain and then put together a total solution rather than individual products.

They do this using the pain sequence.

They begin with questions which find out about the customer's situation, their client base, their challenges, their competitors etc.

Once they have information, and remember good salespeople know all about the customer's industry, competitors etc., and are at the cutting edge of developments.

They then ask questions that reveal problems and issues being experienced. They explore the causes of these and develop hypothetical effects of the problems being experienced long term.

The result? The customer readily shares their challenges and problems to you, allowing you to develop solutions to take this away.

Example questions to problem solve

Situation

- What is…
- When do you..
- Can you tell me about…
- Where do you….
- Who does…
- How do you….
- How is current trading going..
- Where do you see you business going over the next five years?
- What is your corporate plan for….
- How do you view the…..
- How do you assess opportunities…..
- How do you assess barriers…..
- Who are the key people in your business…
- Who are your key people, customers / suppliers…
- What are you general terms…..

Problems

- What are the key issues facing the business at present?
- What are you concerned about….
- What problems does this cause you?
- What difficulties are you having…
- Does the competition give you a problem?
- In what areas do your competitors cause you a problem…
- What kind of problems…
- What are the barriers to achieving….
- Are you satisfied with….
- Does it….help
- How does it….. help
- Where else could it…. help
- Would it be beneficial / useful…

- What benefit would it be to you to resolve…
- How would it be beneficial / useful…
- Where else would it be beneficial / useful…
- Would it help if….
- How would it help….
- Where else would it help…
- Are we saying you want to do something about…..Does that cause you concern…
- How do you feel about that…
- Are you happy with…. Are you comfortable with….
- What is your main concern….
- How important is it that…
- What if…
- What is the effect of this…
- What are the consequences of…
- How does / will that effect…
- How damaging would that be for /to…
- What are the implications of….
- What would happen if….
- Would that result in…
- What impact does that have…
- Could that result in….

Desire for Solution

- Does it….help
- How does it….. help
- Where else could it…. help
- Would it be beneficial / useful…
- What benefit would it be to you to resolve…
- How would it be beneficial / useful…
- Where else would it be beneficial / useful…
- Would it help if….
- How would it help….
- Where else would it help…

Buying Signals on The Phone

These are strong signs from your customer that they are thinking about owning your product or using your service. The thought is in their head. They like what you've said so far, they trust you and your company and are interested.

Traffic lights

Let's look at a system to help you gauge the customer's buying position. Lots of successful salespeople use an imaginary traffic light in their head. You know the classic red, amber and green.

The red light indicates stop. In a car we do this and in selling we should do so as well. The reason is that the customer is not interested and is showing negative signs.

Our actions should be based around bringing the customer out of this negative point of view, if we can.

Amber indicates caution. Proceed carefully and be aware of oncoming traffic. In selling we should do the same. Be aware that we're not quite hitting their buttons yet and should do some more work on this before going too much further.

Green is go, so continue as you're doing. If you've got green towards the end then close and get the paperwork done. Just do it.

Let's look at how we can recognise different colours on our traffic lights.

The red light

When you notice a red light get out of it quickly

"Is everything fine so far?"

"What're your thoughts?"

Or the classic…

"How do you feel about what I've been saying?"

The amber light

Usually a sign something is wrong somewhere and we need to investigate. Ask testing questions to test the temperature. Listen to their thoughts and reactions and act accordingly.

You can usually recognise amber when you're not getting green light signals which we'll look at in a moment and you're not getting red light signals either. You're in the middle.

"What's on your mind Bob?"

"I can see something is on your mind."

Sometimes the best thing to do here is to continue. It could be their way of behaving. Cautious, nervous could be their natural style. Listen to their reactions though. Ask some questions. Get them talking.

"What's on your mind so far?"

"How do you feel about this so far?"

"Is this interesting for you?"

"How does this compare with…?"

The green light

Spotting the green light is very reassuring isn't it? When we are in the middle of the call, it gives us permission to proceed and enjoy ourselves. Towards the end it allows us to close effortlessly and quickly.

The biggest problem I've noticed over the years with salespeople is that some of the more subtle signals are not noticed. Let's look at these.

Verbal signals are a little more tricky so listen carefully. Generally talking faster in a more excited way.

Lots of questions around the product.

"When could you get that agreed?"

"Can I make changes later on?"

"What's the 24/7 support like?"

"What do you think of them?"

"I like the way it does that."

What do you do with their green light? Close them. Maybe a trial such as:

"If everything sounds right for you…let's talk about a case that you're working on then, shall we? "

Presenting on the Phone

Visualise your customer

Walking around call centres watching the people on the phone can be a fascinating experience but the ones that amaze me are those that are acting as though the customer was sitting right there in front of them.

Intrigued was I with one chap so I sat down with him to do some one to one coaching. Sure enough the first call he made he was gesturing, using his hands to describe things, expressing his face, nodding, smiling…it's as though the customer was right there.

During the de-brief I mentioned how impressed I was that he used the pause technique and he spilled out why he does it.

"Simple" he began, "it helps me to communicate and it allows me to give the customer the same experience they would have if I were face to face. It really works for me."

And it did, I commented to him that his voice was richer, he accentuated phrases, he sounded enthusiastic, he listened attentively, and didn't once talk over the customer who was almost hypnotised by his style.

So the tip here is to imagine that your customer is right there in front of you…about 5 or 6 feet away. Don't be afraid to use your hands and gesture to express yourself, and even stand up if it helps.

Words that sell

Without the ability to see and use body language to help communicate, telephone users have to enhance their vocal and verbal skills to make up for this deficiency.

Much has been said about vocal skills already so let's have a look at the language that you use to present information to your customer.

Experts estimate that the average educated person knows about 20,000 words, but only uses 2,000 words regularly. We tend to use the same words over and over again.

So the tip is to expand your vocabulary but before you go and swallow a dictionary, let's not get carried away and start learning words which no one understands. No, use this opportunity to start using more positive words in your telephone speak.

Positive words sound better, feel exciting, motivate your listener and help you to get across ideas in a powerful fashion.

Here's a massive list of 350 words which are positive in nature. How about picking up one a day and use it deliberately 9 times during the day in your conversation. Do this every day for the next year and you'll have increased your positive language vocabulary.

Absolutely	Absorbing	Abundance	Ace
Active	Admirable	Adore	Agree
Alert	A1	Alive	Amazing
Appealing	Approval	Aroma	Attraction
Award	Bargain	Beaming	Beats
Beautiful	Best	Better	Bits
Boost	Bounce	Breakthrough	Breezy
Brief	Bright	Brilliant	Brimming
Buy	Care	Certain	Charming
Chic	Choice	Clean	Clear
Colourful	Comfy	Compliment	Confidence
Connoisseur	Cool	Courteous	Coy
Creamy	Crisp	Cuddly	Dazzling
Debonair	Delicate	Delicious	Delightful
Deluxe	Dependable	Desire	Diamond
Difference	Dimple	Discerning	Distinctive
Divine	Dreamy	Drool	Dynamic
Easy	Economy	Ecstatic	Effervescent
Efficient	Endless	Energy	Enhance

Enjoy	Enormous	Ensure	Enticing
Essence	Essential	Exactly	Excellent
Exceptional	Exciting	Exclusive	Exhilaration
Exotic	Expert	Exquisite	Extol
Extra	Eye-catching	Fabled	Fair
Famous	Fantastic	Fashionable	Fascinating
Fab	Fast	Favourite	Fetching
Finest	Finesse	First	Fizz
Flair	Flattering	Flip	Flourishing
Foolproof	Forever	Fragrance	Free
Freshness	Friendly	Full	Fun
Galore	Generous	Genius	Gentle
Giggle	Glamorous	Glitter	Glorious
Glowing	Go-ahead	Golden	Goodness
Gorgeous	Graceful	Grand	Great
Guaranteed	Happy	Healthy	Heart-warming
Heavenly	Ideal	Immaculate	Impressive
Incredible	Inspire	Instant	Interesting
Invigorating	Invincible	Inviting	Irresistible
Jewel	Joy	Juicy	Keenest
Kind	Kissable	K.O.	Know-how

Leads	Legend	Leisure	Light
Lingering	Logical	Longest	Lovely
Lucky	Luscious	Luxurious	Magic
Matchless	Magnifies it	Maxi	Memorable
Mighty	Miracle	Modern	More
Mouth-watering	Multi	Munchy	Natural
Need	New	Nice	Nutritious
O.K.	Opulent	Outlasts	Outrageous
Outstanding	Palate	Palatial	Paradise
Pamper	Passionate	Peak	Pearl
Perfect	Pick-me-up	Pleasure	Pleases
Plenty	Plum	Plump	Plus
Popular	Positive	Power	Precious
Prefer	Prestige	Priceless	Pride
Prime	Prize	Protection	Proud
Pure	Quality	Quantity	Quenching
Quick	Quiet	Radiant	Ravishing
Real	Reap	Recommend	Refined
Refreshing	Relax	Reliable	Renowned
Reputation	Rest	Rewarding	Rich
Right	Rosy	Royal	Safety

Save	Satisfaction	Scores	Seductive
Select	Sensitive	Sensational	Serene
Service	Sexy	Shapely	Share
Sheer	Shy	Silent	Silver
Simple	Singular	Sizzling	Skilful
Slick	Smashing	Smiles	Solar
Smooth	Soft	Sound	Sparkling
Special	Spectacular	Speed	Spicy
Splendid	Spice	Spotless	Spruce
Star	Strong	Stunning	Stylish
Subtle	Success	Succulent	Sun
Superb	Superlative	Supersonic	Supreme
Sure	Sweet	Swell	Symphony
Tan	Tangy	Tasty	Tempting
Terrific	Thoroughbred	Thrilling	Thriving
Timeless	Tingle	Tiny	Top
Totally	Traditional	Transformation	Treat
Treasure	Trendy	True	Trust
Ultimate	Ultra	Unbeatable	Unblemished
Undeniably	Undoubtedly	U (you)	Unique
Unquestionably	Unrivalled	Unsurpassed	Valued

Valuable	Vanish	Varied	Versatile
Victor	Vigorous	Vintage	V.I.P.
Vital	Vivacious	Warm	Wealth
Wee	Whiz	Whole	Whopper
Winner	Wise	Wonderful	Worthy
Wow!	Youthful	Yule	Young
Zap	Zeal	Zest	Zip

Phrases that don't sell

We've all got our favourite phrases and words which we can over do on occasions, but my pet hate phrase is "to be honest".

I used to use it myself until a customer turned around to me and said.

"So up to now then you've been lying have you…."

Using this phrase adds nothing to the sentence – it's plain negative.

So examine your language and the kind of phrases you use regularly and eliminate them as soon as you can. Here's some more examples of the impact they might have on your customers:

- Expressions that suggest carelessness
    - "You neglected to specify…"
    - "You failed to include…"
    - "You overlooked enclosing…"
- Expressions that imply that the recipient is not too bright (ow!)
    - "We cannot see how you…"
    - "We fail to understand…"
    - "We are at a loss to know…"
- Demanding phrases that imply coercion/pressure
    - "You should…"

- "You ought to..."
- "You must..."

- Phrases that might be interpreted as sarcastic or patronising

    - "No doubt..."
    - "We will thank you to..."
    - "You understand, of course..."
    - "Please respond soon..."

Rid yourself of tainted words

Are you a fan of 80s music? I'm a big fan. Read on to discover how a 1980s band can help you with your tainted words.

The other night I was watching some 1980s videos on VH1. I came across one of my favourite bands – Soft Cell and their number one hit "Tainted Love" originally released in 1981.

And it got me thinking about other tainted things. Tainted words came to mind and I came up with four tainted words to banish.

Tainted...contaminated...stained...infected.

These are some words that you really want to stop using in your sales and coaching language but they just seem to pop up everywhere.

Signature

Please sign here. Sign your life away you mean. Just stop and think of the impact this has on people. It can terrify some, turn others in to objection maniacs or just stop others in their tracks to really question what they're doing.

Think of alternative ways of asking people to sign things. Use autograph, "Can you authorise this for me please", "Can you kindly OK this for me please"

If you indicate to the customer where they should be signing keep well away from putting an X marks the spot and use a tick instead. What does the note X mean to people?

Yep it means wrong, zip, zero, bad, you can do better, incorrect.

Obvious when you think about it.

Problems

Use this word at your peril. I often talk about revealing customer problems before introducing a solution and this is a tried and tested consultative selling technique. Just don't use the word "problem". Instead use challenge or issue.

Price

Definitely a no-no. Cheap, even worse and you'll be inviting discounts. Instead re-phrase to cost, investment or fee. They just sound better.

Hesitate

We use the phrase "Don't hesitate to contact me". What are people going to do first? Yes they're going to hesitate before calling you, so they won't call you.

So there we have four tainted words – I'm sure you can think of some more of your own. Let's banish them to the video archives of the early 1980's with those dreadful hairstyles.

Leave off the pounds

Here's a little tip to help you put across a cost figure which may seem a lot of money. To make it sound less than it is, just leave off the pound.

For example "My fee is one thousand two hundred pounds".

Or

"My fee is one thousand two hundred".

It just sounds less.

Help them visualise using it

Last night I was watching a programme on the TV which involved a young couple who had to make a big choice when it came to buying a new home.

One home was in the French Atlantic coastline, a beautiful stretch of land glistening in the warmth of the sunshine. The house was fantastic, 4 bedrooms, sun terrace and full of original features.

The other place was in Exmouth in Devon, equally sublime but didn't share the same climate. It was a two bedroom terrace Victorian house with a garden overlooked by plenty of others.

Two estate agents covered each region and you would have thought the French one would have won hands down because of the location and property. But no, the Exmouth agent just had a knack of presenting his property better.

He continually helped the couple to imagine what it would be like living there, what would they use the garden for, who they would invite to the barbeques, when would they nip down to the sea, where would they fit their furniture…and so on.

Once they'd had the tour of the property in Exmouth, they could see themselves living there.

Now the poor agent in France did none of this. She pointed out good features but just kept on talking and talking and talking.

You can guess which one they chose.

So think about how you present your product or solution and help your customer to own it. Help them to visualise how they would use it.

Cross Selling

5 cross selling techniques

Everywhere you look, cross selling is alive and kicking but it's usually online and automated. Tesco sporting its specials when you do your online shop, Amazon suggesting you might also like this, the sports site bundling the pump with your shiny new soccer ball.

But when you go face to face with salespeople, we seem to have an aversion to cross sell. Perhaps we're worried about being too pushy or salesey, after all, websites don't have feelings but people do and having a customer reject you might put you off offering your additional product to the next customer.

Here are 5 strategies that'll help you cross sell more without the worry of rejection or annoying your customer.

Problem questions

We all know that the secret to consultative selling is finding out the customer's challenges, problems, pains that motivate them to want to buy our product or service so as to relieve themselves of the pain they're suffering. Of course, there's more to selling than just plugging pains, but it certainly creates motivation to act.

The secret here is to craft some questions to ask your customer that reveal the pains and challenges they face and maybe hadn't realised, so you can present your product to solve them. That's cross selling. Here's how.

Take an inventory of what you sell and note down the problems that they solve. Every product or service solves an issue, a problem – you just have to find it. For example credit cards, everyone's current enemy number one, solve the problem of short term need for cash. So if you're arranging a loan for a customer, rather than harping on about the great introductory interest rate, ask a question on how your customer copes with short term cash flow crises. That way a credit card might be appealing.

Alternatively you could use this technique. Suggest the problem and ask how they're coping with the problem. For example:

"Many of our customers struggle to keep the hardwood floors clean; may I ask how you're planning to do this?"

"Lots of our customers get into short term cash flow challenges; may I ask how you deal with those?"

Once they have talked about maybe suffering from the problem, you introduce your product and hey presto.

Chunk up the problem

Customers come to you for a product or service and our test is to be able to cross sell. An answer is to chunk up the problem in your customer's mind to something bigger or the big picture challenge. Ask them what the problem is part of. For example:

"I see you're looking to secure some hard wood flooring for the space, can I ask what bigger project is this part of?"

"A loan is important to you to finance the car, if you don't mind me asking, how does this fit in with your overall plan to finance major purchases?"

"You're looking for a great deal on your mortgage, but what's the bigger aim for your family of getting a mortgage?"

Once you have the bigger problem in the air, you can then consider packaging a suite of products to suit the needs. Presenting a package of services and products can help you cross sell by eliminating the "add on" perception that some people have. Rather than adding the shoe polish at the checkout, which is too late, consider a package of products which includes polish, cleaning cloths, warranties and shoes, all at a bulk discount of course.

Something new and shiny

One of my favourite programmes on TV is the Gadget Show on Channel 4. An hour of the newest, shiniest, must have gadgets.

And that's the point about cross selling. Sometimes, as customers, we don't know what the newest, shiniest, must have product is. So salespeople or customer service people mustn't be afraid of just telling them what the latest product is.

Naturally it must be relevant to the customer first and you need to put it across as a brand new offering, something new, and you'll probably get your customer excited.

Here are some more ideas:

Use a customer story to present the "something new" product. Show how a previous customer was initially sceptical and then realised the fabulous benefits once they started to use it. Stories must be real, involve characters, have a challenge to bridge and enjoy a solution at the end.

Use the "are you sure?" approach when they initially baulk at the something new product. A quick "are you sure?" with the right tone, smile and eye contact can often persuade them away from their knee jerk reaction to being presented something else.

Bundling

Use the "Amazon – others found this product to be useful too" approach of bundling products together. Amazon are world renowned for this cross selling strategy and it works as people are influenced about what others say or do. Mention that many of your customers also found this product of benefit as well. This bundling of products approach can work really well if you've done your homework on what you sell.

Can you link them together in some way, do they complement each other, and have similar benefits?

The right beliefs

It's all in the head. Cross selling for some is an anathema, an abomination, a loathing. But to others it's the natural order of things, something to cherish as you're helping the customer solve their problems and satisfy their needs.

To some it's natural, to others it's a dreadful experience.

And how you feel will determine how successful you are.

So rid your mind of negative beliefs when it comes to cross selling. Adopt a higher purpose in your selling or customer service role. Convince yourself that what you are doing is moral, designed to help the customer and a valuable service.

Here are the 4 empowering beliefs of successful cross sellers. They believe:

1. Serving the customer is good

2. Customers actually want our products and services – all of them

3. Customers want my expertise and cross selling helps me to demonstrate this

4. Customers can say no if they want, I'm ok with that.

Adopt them. Use the 21 day rule if you like, write them on cards and read them out to yourself every day for 21 days and you'll begin to believe in them.

Or just realise that if you don't, then you will never succeed at cross selling continuously.

After all websites don't have feelings, and they're super successful at cross selling – just ask Amazon whose cross selling engine generates 40% of their total sales revenue – that's computer code, not a human.

Closing the Sale

ABC – Always Be Closing

One of my favourite films – Glengarry Glen Ross – a tale of the goings on in a real estate office, involved Alec Baldwin giving one of the most impressive sales training lessons ever. He ranted the ABC – Always Be Closing. Look it up on YouTube, it's famous.

Maybe slightly 1980s cheese, but the concept is true today. Closing the sale doesn't have a great reputation amongst salespeople because we often leave it too late, at the end of the sales process when the pressure's on and the heat's evident. It's this fear of rejection or annoying the customer that stops us from doing it.

Maybe Alec Baldwin, or Blake in the movie, had an idea with his ABC. Let me share with you 5 strategies that might help you do the ABC of closing.

Signpost them to a close

Most things in life have a process to follow, even shopping at your local supermarket. The first part of the shopping process is parking the car safely before entering the store. But at Sainsbury's in Cheltenham last Saturday morning, this was a big challenge. A new store had opened opposite so the car park was packed. Sainsbury's re-deployed some staff members with giant signs to guide customers to where the spaces were.

Clever really because Sainsbury's were signposting the customer along their sales process. The first part was to park, the second to gather a trolley and so on.

In the same way, when your customer makes contact, put them onto your sales process and guide them along it. Tell them what you are going to do; the benefits – let the conveyor belt do its job and guide them to a close.

A favourite of mine is to encourage the customer to appreciate that at some point you're going to ask them if they want to go ahead. Alleviate their fears if it helps, by stating that they don't have to go ahead today, but if they wish, they can do so. This is very non-threatening and a super way of progressing to a close.

Ticks of approval

Alec Baldwin's mantra – the ABC – Always Be Closing – rings true since waiting until the end of the sales process can conjure up the close as a giant hurdle to cross. Instead break the close down into smaller closes and ask for the "tick of approval" to move onto the next phase of your sales cycle. Ask your customer for permission to move forward, gain their tick of approval.

Break down your sales process into milestones that need a tick of approval. For example, the first stage might be a meeting to discuss needs. Once the customer has agreed to this, that's a tick of approval. Early in my sales process is the qualifying stage. I need to secure the MAN – their motivation, their ability and their needs – before I proceed. Once I have these safe, that's a tick of approval and my process continues.

Break down the sales process into tick points or where the customer needs to take some action or give you some important information towards their purchase.

By nailing your ticks of approval will gradually move the customer to the natural conclusion, the close, with little or no fuss.

Testing trials

Test and trial closing go back to my first days in sales in the early 1980s and didn't have a good name then. But the concept is sound; after all, asking for the business suddenly without warning can be dangerous to your health. And the customer's too.

There's not a better day out than spending it at the seaside. The sand, the sunshine and the sea. The 3 S's. But here in the UK, even on a warm summer's day, the sea can be terrifyingly cold. The secret is to gradually immerse yourself in the waves, an inch at a time until your entire body is submerged and you can dive into the depths.

Some people prefer to just run into the waves and dive straight it. After an initial shock and awe, they emerge victorious but it does look terrifying from my position, I'd prefer to gradually immerse myself. I also think most customers would prefer that we gradually close them rather than all at once.

Test closes are a neat way to slowly immerse yourself in the cold sea. "How does that sound?" "Would that be useful?" "What do you think so far?"

Watch for their reaction, any reservations at this early stage can swiftly be ironed out. Likewise if the sea is really cold, you can easily withdraw to the sanctuary of the towel.

Trial closes are just a little bit more to the point and make a suggestion to the customer of moving forward. "If we were in a position to move forward, would that be a good next step?" "If I can get the paperwork moving on this, would you be in a position to move forward?"

Finally, ask for their commitment but do it in a questions format:

"We're in agreement aren't we, so what's your next step?" "Any more questions or are you ready to go ahead?" "How can we make this happen?" "We could get the ball rolling in August…what would you like me to do?"

Using convincer triples

Did you know that during the night-time, we actually lose weight? Also during the working day, we shrink, only by millimetres admittedly and the weight loss is only grams. And the last one is amazing; no one person's hands are identical in size.

All good things come in triples; after all I am the middle child! Triples are a way of giving information or persuading people, in packets of three. Three is a magic number so use triples when closing or gaining some form of commitment.

Information delivered in threes has a hypnotic effect and ensures acceptance.

Deliver two agreed phrases before you ask for the business. Two convincers. For example. "This all looks ideal doesn't it and the investment is well within your budget, so do you think we ought to go ahead."

"The paperwork is all done, you've chosen your preferred hard-wood, it's all within budget, so let's move forward shall we?"

Convincer, convincer, close.

Known as the 3 part convincer in NLP circles, I call it smooth closing and by the way, everyone's hands are identical in size.

Pose as the expert

Take control, after all, you are the expert aren't you. Simply suggest that we move forward and you could combine this with a yes tag if you want to be really eloquent.

"It's all fitting together isn't it, so I recommend we crack on, shall we?"

"This really suits you doesn't it, I'm thinking we ought to get cracking now."

Maybe Alec was right – ABC – Always Be Closing – although the phrase does have a 1980s ring to it, not applicable to today's in control customer. The secret is to subtly always be closing, making it smooth, almost unnoticed, so we can close more business with customers who have a genuine need for our services and products.

Question the close

Here's an alternative way to close the sale when selling on the telephone.

It's all to do with asking questions which, of course, is the best way to keep control and casually guide the customer along the process.

Use questions to ask the customer what he or she wants to do next. Here are some examples:

"We're in agreement then aren't we? What's the next step?"

And my favourite…

- "Any more questions or are you ready to go ahead?"
- "How can we make this happen?"
- "We could start this in August…what would you like me to do?"

So get used to asking questions to close the sale, they work particularly well on the phone.

Are you sure?

Last week I was in the City of London working with a stockbroker client helping their salespeople get more business using the phones. Impressive environment it was. Exciting, positive, energetic, fast-paced. And I just adored the myriad of computer screens everywhere showing stock figures and enormous amounts of data. Their job was just so cool.

On my way home I dreamt of being a real life stockbroker but as I arrived in Gloucester, reality hit me and realised the closest I'd ever get would be having more than one computer screen in my office.

So the next morning, I put my revised ambition into action and headed down to PC World to buy a second monitor. In its glorious 22 inches it was surprisingly inexpensive. I rushed to the checkout.

I always feel for the checkout operators with their targets to sell add on insurances and warranties. The problem with selling add-ons is…well they're add-ons, and no one wants costs added. The checkout is not the place to do selling either, with queues and finger drumming customers. Until I reached Naomi.

"You'll be wanting the 3 year Warranty… won't you?"

"No thanks"

"Are you sure" she replied with a genuine look of surprise. She contorted her face and mirrored shock and astonishment; she'd obviously practised this many times in the training room.

"These monitors can go wrong after the manufacturer's warranty and you'd be missing out on a free fix for another two years if it goes wrong…are you sure? "

She was very persuasive and what a clever little strategy.

So if you or your team sell "add-ons" at the checkout or counter and they're often busy and harassed, follow Naomi's example.

1.   Use the Yes tag…"you'd like…wouldn't you?"

2.   When the customer says no…look genuinely surprised, "are you sure?"

3.   Give a benefit they'd be missing and try again.

Brilliant. I levelled with Naomi and told her I was a sales trainer and asked her how successful she was. Very, was her reply. It was inertia that encouraged the customers to go for the add-on, a few took it straight away but more reacted positively to the "are you sure?"

My office looks great with the two monitors as I dream of being a stockbroker. At least my time management has improved, it really has. You ought to try two monitors but beware of Naomi at the checkout.

The Rhythm is going to get you

When we're selling or persuading or trying to convince someone on anything, we should be thinking the rhythm of three. We should try and always give 3 reasons for a customer to buy your product and you'll be more persuasive.

Why? Because rhythms of 3 are more elegant and more convincing than rhythms of 2 or 4. They just are.

Try doing a rhythm of 3 sales close.

"So you like this benefit,

And you really felt that part was great

And the delivery date really suits you.

Shall we go ahead today then?"

Works doesn't it? Elegant. Also remember to place your most important benefit or argument at the end as this gives it more power and is more believable. Everything should come in a rhythm of 3.

Gloria Estafan sang "The rhythm is going to get you" way back in the 1980s.

The rhythm of 3 stills holds true today.

Handling Customers with Problems

Removing the emotion

Have you ever had to deal with customer problems and queries particularly when they start getting a little heated? Your blood pressure builds, you start becoming defensive – all those human emotions of dealing with stressful situations can get in the way of handling the issue competently.

I took up mini rugby refereeing a couple of years ago and experienced this many times. Occasionally when I made a decision which went against the coaches' and parents' views, I began to feel pressure build up inside especially when the same parents voiced their concern over my decision.

This blood pressure build up clouded my concentration and affected the way I went about the rest of the match.

In the same way handling intense customer problems where they might be a little agitated can have a similar effect.

I improved my knowledge of rugby laws, took some courses and this knowledge helped me. Likewise we can ensure our own product knowledge, understanding of the computer system and general confidence can help us to handle customer problems.

But the real breakthrough for me came when I heard these words from an experienced referee:

"Be sure of yourself, take your time, move purposely, act deliberately, be decisive with your communication, ignore the calls from the touchline, blur them out of your mind and above all remember that there is no game without the referee."

This strategy advice changed my game enormously and removed many of the emotions.

Like a lot of difficult situations the best thing to do is to plan in advance how you're going to tackle them when they occur. You'll be amazed at how quickly this can take the pressure off the moment and let you deal with the situation deliberately and professionally without emotions getting in the way.

LAPAC Strategy

- L - listen
- A - Acknowledge
- P - Probe

- A - Answer
- C – Confirm

Listen

Telephone listening needs to be noisier than the face to face kind. Let the customer spill out their problem or issue and invite them to empty out before moving onto the next stage.

Use verbal nods to show you're listening "I see", "go on".

Concentrate on the caller and try to eliminate any distractions around you, both external ones and those that go on inside. Remove the emotions that might be building up inside you. Remember the customer is not getting excited with you, just the company you work for.

Get yourself into 3rd person position to build empathy; this is where you can see both your and the customer's point of view. Then you'll appreciate their excitement.

Finally remember to summarise the problem that they customer has given you using a phrase such as "Let me make sure I've got this right then…"

Acknowledge

More empathy building going on here. Acknowledge that you've heard, have understood and can see their point of view. This is often enough to placate them until you've solved the problem as it buys you time.

Use reflective statements here such as:

"I understand what you're saying."

"I can appreciate how you feel about that."

"I've been through that as well and it was terrible."

"I see where you're coming from."

"Gosh that must be awful."

Probe

Now's your opportunity to probe a little more to ensure you have the situation clear in your mind. Ask some searching questions to isolate the problem or issue to make sure you have it all wrapped up. Asking a question or two also gives you valuable thinking time so you can chew over the problem a little more.

Take care with your questioning though, as deliberate precise questioning can be construed as interrogation and if your customer is getting a little irate this can turn up their blood pressure.

Use open questions here and soften them by putting a soft fronter to them. Sometimes just by putting a few words at the beginning of a question can really soften its impact and make it far more palatable. Words such as:

"May I ask…."

"I'd be curious to know…."

"I'd be very interested to know…"

"Tell me…"

Or any other words that suit your style.

Telephone experts usually have a full voice range able to effortlessly move from low to high pitch at will. Most of us have to learn this. Deliver a question by lifting your voice a tiny bit at the end of the question.

Answer

Now's the time to answer the customer's issue or problem. It may be that you'll have to go away and find out, speak to someone else or whatever is needed to get the answer. Make sure you obey the golden rule of under promising and over delivering. Give a timescale to get back to them but allow yourself some buffer just in case.

Sometimes you have to give bad news and here's some ideas to deal with this particularly difficult task, which many of us dread and will put off.

Three steps to give bad news:

1. Tell the truth
2. Reflect feelings
3. Take charge for the next step

Tell the truth as it is. Don't flower it up to make it sound less imposing. Get to the point and give the facts and use as little language as you can. Don't waffle the answer.

You can mix up the bad news with some good news using the word "but" to separate them. "But" puts emphasis on the next part of the sentence for example:

"I'm afraid our product doesn't have that feature but it does allow for unlimited claims in the future."

"Your claw back period will be 3 years but once you've achieved this level of business we can reduce this to 1 year."

Then reflect feelings which you'll get. Go silent. Wait and they will respond. Reflect, reflect, reflect but be careful you don't agree, just respect their position and situation.

Once you've reflected feelings, launch into next step mode. Your customer will want to hear what's the next step so take charge and outline where you can go from here and what can be done in the future. Think actions.

Confirm

Finally confirm that all is OK or that you've helped as much as you can.

LAPAC is really useful and does work. The key parts are the acknowledging and probing which calms your customer and gives you thinking time. It shows the customer that we want to take some time with their issue and do what we can to help.

Use it, practise it and next time you find yourself getting high blood pressure, just stick to the strategy and you'll soon find the emotions leaving and you can concentrate on answering the query or handling the problem. Just as I now do with my little junior rugby players when the coaches and parents start debating my decisions on the pitch. But I have to say the little ones are darlings on the pitch, it's the parents who sometimes need to do some growing up.

Rant over!

Objection Handling

Pre-empting Objections

How can a holiday home jog your memory about how to handle objections in selling?

Well, this year on holiday with my family, I was reminded how effective the pre-empting technique is. It was a scorching afternoon in the Vendee, France at Les Dunes Camping Site. We'd just arrived after a long drive and Sharon, our rep, was showing us to our caravan which was to be home for a few weeks. Now this is always a scary moment as you are in their hands for the choice of location.

Would we be next to the family from hell?

Would we be next to the bar or worse still, the Karaoke?

No, we were being led back towards the entrance to the park, with the main road and amusements. Before I even thought of the noise issue, the rep turned around and said confidently.

"The people before you were a little worried about being close to the entrance but when they left yesterday they told me what a great location they had. They mentioned how close the van was to all the amenities and how quiet it was at night."

I hadn't even thought about the noise problem until she mentioned it but because she'd given me a customer testimonial and some benefits of the location, it didn't even cross my mind that it would be a quandary.

Clever girl.

I wonder if she was a trained salesperson? But the point was she did just the right thing. Let me explain further.

No product or service is perfect. There's always downsides or disadvantages or the competition has the edge in one or two areas. No one has a "killer application" for long these days as competition is so swift and reactive.

There's always going to be something the customer might not fully appreciate and just might lead to an objection later on, usually when we ask for the order or close the sale.

Now I'm not saying that you should tell the customer all the main problems of your product early on in the process. What I'm saying is, if there is a particular feature that the competition beats you on, and previous customers have mentioned it before, then pre-empt it.

Just like Sharon did with the caravan location.

It might not be a problem with your product or service. It could be just a hurdle your customer has to cross before they can enjoy the product. Something that potentially might cause them to stall when it comes to purchasing.

Seek out your product deficiencies, if you don't know then ask your competition as they'll be sure to let you know! Then think of a way of making the disadvantage or potential problem not seem such a big deal early on in your sales process.

Some examples to assist you. Say X was an issue. You could use Sharon's technique with a customer testimonial.

"One thing about our product is X, however only yesterday I had a letter from a customer who really found this to be a benefit to them.. I'd be happy share the letter with you."

"Naturally you have to think of X, but what this really means to you is incredible peace of mind."

Notice that the words "however" and "but" really emphasise the second part of the sentence, which is what I want to do.

Price is sometimes an issue. Maybe your product or service is on the pricy side. Now price is merely a reflection of value. If there are enough benefits to the customer, then the price is merely what needs to be paid to achieve the value. If we don't pile on the benefits to the customer, then they won't always see the value.

But if price can seem to encourage a "How muuuch!" response, break it down into bite sized chunks. This morning I was downloading some songs from an online retailer and they were trying to sell me their monthly instalment plan so I could download 25 tracks a month. Cleverly they'd made the point that each track would cost me less than 30p and compared to other sites who charge 80p or more, this sounded really good.

If your product is payable monthly such as life assurance or health insurance, be sure to break it down into a daily cost. People aren't stupid and we should never do it for this reason – it just sounds better.

There's a few ideas to assist you but I'm sure at this stage you're thinking of your proposal and how to pre-empt potential objections at an early stage.

Another story I heard whilst on holiday was Virgin Money's decision to offer staff ebreaks. You see call centre staff at their offices were taking time out from making calls to check social media, YouTube etc. It got to such a proportion that the managers gave all staff a 15 minute ebreak during the day so they can do their social media.

Clever.

You can't stop staff doing it, so build time in the day for it to happen so you can control it.

Remember, think of your product or service, seek out the problems or deficiencies and build ways into your sales process to pre-empt the issue, so it doesn't become a problem later on.

By the way, the caravan location was perfect and I heard my wife explain to Sharon that we'd had a wonderful few weeks and would like the same spot next time.

Knee jerk reactions

As a kid, I was fascinated when doctors would carefully tap a patient's knee with a small hammer and the patient's leg would involuntary kick upwards. That's where the phrase "knee jerk reaction" comes from. For years after first seeing this on TV, I tried in vain to make my knee do the same with plenty of bruises to show for my efforts.

Life is full of knee jerk reactions. People get used to reacting in a certain way especially when they are being offered to buy something. You see, when faced with a decision to buy something, we will revert to a knee jerk reaction and say something like, "No thanks" or "I'll think about it" or "Send/email me some brochures."

Unfortunately many salespeople or those on the front line who need to sell things, accept these customer reactions and don't close on the sale.

And this is a shame because they are often not real reasons.

The secret is to accept them for what they are…knee jerk reactions and kind of ignore them and try again. Throw in a holding phrase and re-do your close. If done carefully and subtly, it won't harm and may get the customer to think it through again and make a positive decision.

Some favourite responses that won't offend:

"That's fine, I'm only asking for a short chat with our adviser, it won't harm will it?"

"I understand, however the benefits are excellent…."

"Are you sure? You'll be missing out on…"

"I could email you some brochures but I've a better idea, let's meet shortly to talk it through…"

Bear in mind a customer's first reaction to your close, is normally a "no" because this is an in-built knee jerk reaction.

The second, more significant knee jerk reaction comes from us, the salesperson. When a customer gives us an objection or reservation which might be entirely understandable and realistic, we immediately come in with a pre-thought through answer to the objection, especially if we've just come back from a training course and we know all the answers to common objections.

Again the trick is to react differently. A nifty little reminder here is to imagine sitting on their lap. Of course, this is a metaphor and not something to actually do, although that depends on your customer I guess. No, I'm saying we follow the LAP rule – L for listen to the reservation and really hear them out first, then we A acknowledge it. I'm not saying agree with them but see their point of view, understand where they're coming from. And the final P is to probe to figure out exactly what it is they have an issue with.

"I can see where you're coming from there and it's a fine point you're making…can I just ask…is that the only issue that might prevent you going ahead with this plan?"

This strategy gives you thinking time, ensures your customer knows they're being listened to and shows you're on their side.

So consider the two knee jerk reactions the next time you're in a sales situation. The customer's reaction to your close and your potential quick response to their reservation. Both hazardous in their own right.

And try as a may, I still can't get my knee to kick upwards every time I whack it with a hammer. Maybe if I hit it harder…

Some more objection handling scripts

I'm not interested

"I understand Bob, and I'm sure you get a lot of these kinds of calls don't you? Well I do too, and believe me I don't like getting them any more than you do. But I'll tell you, every now and then I listen to one because it turns out to be something really good that ends up benefiting me – and this is one of those calls for you today.

Let me ask you one thing…" (now ask about a problem you know they are having)

I want to think about it

"You know Bob, whenever I say that to a sales rep I really mean one of three things. I either don't fully understand it, or I'm interested but not sold on it yet, or the timing isn't right or something else. Please be honest, which is it for you?"

Now hit mute.

"That's fine, I'm only asking for a short chat, it won't harm and it will make a difference to your business."

Now hit mute.

We're happy where we are

"That's great Bob, that tells me you understand the value of a solid solution for this. In fact you're exactly the kind of company we work with. You see, I'm not suggesting you stop using what's working for you, but rather I'm here to help you get even better. You see the companies that use us as well have found that they can decrease their costs by …

"And to see if this will work for you as well, let me just ask you a couple of quick questions."

"I'm with you on that one, you'll only want to switch your provider if it's a better deal and its proven to be so. Can I ask a question? If I provided you with proof, would you seriously consider switching?"

Now hit the mute button.

Just email me something

"I'd be happy to, but a quick question if I may, and please be totally honest with me, is it a priority for you in the next 30 days to do something here? "

Now hit the mute button.

Handling the price objection

The next time you have a customer who is objecting to your price for your product or service, here's a little quotation that'll remind you how business works.

"It is unwise to pay too much, but it is unwise to pay too little. When you pay too much you lose a little money and that is all, but when you pay too little you sometimes lose everything, because the thing that you have bought isn't capable of doing the thing which it was bought to do."

"The common law of business balance prohibits you from paying a little and receiving a lot – it can't be done. If you deal with the lowest bidder it would be as well to add something from the risk you run, and if you can so that you can afford to buy something better."

John Ruskin 1819 – 1900

How to Write Business Emails

Many of us are writing more and more emails to internal and external customers replacing letters and phone calls. The upshot is that we're receiving more emails than ever before, so how do we cope?

We cope by being selective of the emails we read, we scan headings to determine whether we read it or not, we pay close attention to the sender and often only open it if we know or trust them. We scan the body of the email rather than read. We rarely turn the page over. The "page over" is the bottom of the screen requiring us to scroll down.

A recent survey in the UK stated that 25% of the workforce spends one hour a day on email and from that, 34% of emails are worthless.

Makes you think doesn't it?

To help you write the perfect email to your customers I'm going to show you some best practice tips and strategies that'll help you through the email jungle so your customers get to read and take in your message. I'm going to examine your style of writing, tips on how to compose your email body and finally, what to avoid.

Modern and non-stuffy

The first secret is to be modern and non stuffy in your emails. In business, however, there is no place for smilies and too much informality. Reserve that for email with friends on your Hotmail account. Bear in mind that any email you type could find itself on the front page of The Sun newspaper.

Plain language

The secret is plain language. Simple, short sentences so the reader understands immediately. Rid yourself of your perfect English language ego and get into short sentences, 15 or so words each. Plus short words, one or two syllables is fine. Email readers don't have the patience as letter readers, they are not the same thing, remember people scan emails, they don't study them.

On the subject of plain language, write in an active way. By this I mean write as you would speak to someone personally. For example "You can complete the enrolment online at your leisure" rather than "The enrolment can be completed online". Slightly different but a massive impact. Write as you would speak in the present not the past – it's just so non-stuffy.

Formal versus informal

Formal versus informal. And in the cup final, formal wins by 2 goals to 1. Informality is not for business emails. A survey in 2000 showed that business people were increasingly irritated by the lack of salutations and informality.

Leave the "Hi's" and the "see you's" and the "LOLs" and the "IMHOs" to your Hotmail emails. In business, remember your salutations such as Doctor, Mr, Mrs. OK, if you know them call them by their first name and use "Hello" rather than "Dear". And use "Goodbye" rather than "Yours sincerely", after all we're not in the Victorian age anymore. However, if you don't know them and they are a customer , then use "Dear Mr Brown" and "Yours sincerely" to be on the safe side You can always go from formal to informal – it's like putting on a tie if you don't know how to dress – you can easily take the tie off.

KISS

I have a number of tips and secrets for you on how to actually write your email body. First of all give your customer a big kiss on the cheeks. Of course this is a metaphor rather than a request. KISS stands for keep it short and sweet. Brief, precise and to the point. Just like this paragraph.

I'll keep banging on with the same message. Email readers don't have the same patience as letter readers. The 21st Century and the internet have made us scanners, and top liners. Typically we read for about 5 seconds and click on to the next page. Yes, there are exceptions as your email might be important to them, then again it might not be, and they scan you and ignore you. So keep it short and simple – KISS.

Plan first

Do plan your response first. It's so easy to hit reply and bang on with your reply without thinking about the message since you have dozens of emails to get through. And whilst you're there, you copy and paste similar paragraphs from other letters so as to save time. If you must use templates, put a link in your email to a page on your website that has the information you want them to read, don't paste it into your email body. It simply won't fit. It's like jamming a square peg into a round hole. Besides readers soon pick up on the fact it's a templated return.

Instead, plan your response on paper first. Think of your key points, maybe some headings, think about bullet lists. Consider your subject line to make it compelling. Email readers look at three things to determine whether to open or not.

Your name as the sender needs to be known and trusted, the subject line and finally whether there's an attachment or not. This last one still scares people. The subject line should be unique, it's lazy to leave it as "Re: Request for Enrolment Information". Use "Our reply with the information you wanted".

It works when the email sender has asked you a number of questions, to copy these into the reply and use them as headings, clearly laid out. Summarise the question as a heading and put it into your email as a heading, maybe bold it to show up. Don't underline anything in emails as it is known as a link and might confuse.

Opener

Your opening paragraph should make it clear as to what your email is about and the action you want them to take. For example, if the action is to click somewhere to enrol online, then put this in the opening paragraph. Customers need to be told what to do next.

Paragraphs

Keep them short on emails – a maximum of two sentences. Remember people scan, they don't read. Use headings to help signpost the customer.

Think about using bullets or lists and maybe start this with a short paragraph as a forecast of the bulleted list.

If you provide links, and you should, to create brevity in the email, then put them as separate lines. Try not to hide the link in a word – put the entire web address on the email as people distrust one word links and some email filters will filter your email out.

Numbers

If you use numbers, use the digital form not the long spelling. For example twenty-two should be 22. It's just clearer and simpler and easier to take in quickly.

Call to action

The final paragraph should be a call to action. What is it you want the customer to do next? Do you want them to call you, enrol, buy online, consider the information and contact you when they are ready? Whatever it is, the call to action needs to be at the end. Remember customers need to know what to do next, especially email readers. And don't end with "Please do not hesitate to contact us if you require any further information". What do people do when they read this? Yep, they hesitate…

Instead use "If you want more help or information, please do email me personally, and I'll help you some more"

Proof

Once done, do find the time to proof the email and spell check before pressing send. After all you can't recall an email once it's sent. Now might be the best time for a compelling subject line now that you have the message clear in your head. Many people leave the subject line to the end once they know exactly what the email is going to say.

What to avoid

Here's a list of things to avoid on emails:

- Abbreviations such as LOL, FYI, BBS. Leave those for IM'ing

- Smilies – have no place in business emails :-)

- Exclamation'itis!!!!

- Slang

- Templated replies

- Bulky attachments, in fact if you don't know them, provide a link instead

- Your emotion. By this I mean if you are particularly angry or excited about the email, wait until this subsides otherwise this emotion will come through in the text.

Summary

Emails are a part of life and rightfully so. Some key messages in this article are to keep emails plain, remember KISS, focus on the impatience of readers and write for them and their need to scan. Write in the active voice – plan, don't template.

How to Measure Customer Care with an NPS

What is an NPS – Net Promoter Score?

Any piece of training or development needs to be measured to see what difference it's made. This is the Holy Grail professional trainers have been working towards for decades and for many programmes, it's not that difficult to measure the impact if you start off by deciding your measures before you embark on the training.

But the trickiest one to measure is customer care training; until now that is. The answer, which many organisations I've been working with recently have discovered, is the NPS or Net Promoter Score.

Net Promoter was developed by Fred Reichheld, and detailed in his book "The Ultimate Question".

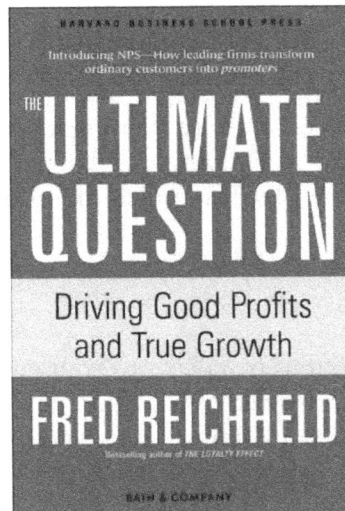

Why an NPS?

Firstly why bother? Simply because you need to know what your customers think of you. Not how great you are, or whether your widgets are the best and your customer response team answers calls in 3 rings.

Customers nowadays are not prepared to answer such detailed questionnaires. But they will be prepared to answer one question…would you be prepared to recommend us to a friend, colleague or associate?

Let me convince you further. Customers are now in control of the buying process, sales people are no longer required in their traditional fashion and many are now being called "talking brochures".

Companies now realise that customers make a decision to buy in two ways. One, they Google the solution they're looking for and secondly, they ask someone in their network if they know of a company that can help.

This asking someone is hugely popular today with the rise of social networking and the celebrated "like" button. Interesting research has proven that people believe customer testimonials even if they haven't met that person.

Personal recommendations have never been more important. So you need to measure this ultimate action from your customers and you can do so with the NPS.

A final thought to convince you to embark on the NPS journey. What gets measured gets done is a famous saying and is so true. So if you measure your customer's reluctance or acceptance of referring you, then you'll do what you can to improve the score.

And did I forget to mention that everyone else is doing it, large and small companies. Siemens, Philips, BP, Tesco, …they're all doing it and some even have the need to measure the NPS amongst their boardroom objectives which filter down to everyone in the organisation.

How can you measure NPS?

How can you measure it? You need to be talking to your customers, or emailing them asking them to complete a brief online survey that takes a minute. Beware of offering incentives; just tell them that you want to constantly improve the service you give them. Most people are happy to work with that.

How you get your customers to do the survey is up to you. You need to do it anonymously, leave out the names, that doesn't matter and don't ask your sales people or customer service people to ask customers as the pressure will be too much for an unbiased response.

Last month, I was at a supermarket checkout and as the lady was scanning my items; on the screen facing me was the message "Would I be inclined to recommend them?" With the cashier's face beaming a wide smile, I was unduly influenced to give my opinion. Instead I didn't bother and smiled back. A clever idea in theory but not in practice.

Emails are best, or it could be a text message, which is another good reason to harvest email addresses and mobiles from customers. With emails you can hyperlink them straight to a survey page.

On the survey page you need to ask them the vital question. "How likely are you to recommend us to a business partner, colleague or friend?" You then give them a 1 to 10 grading, 1 is not likely at all and 10 is a definite.

Let me show you graphically.

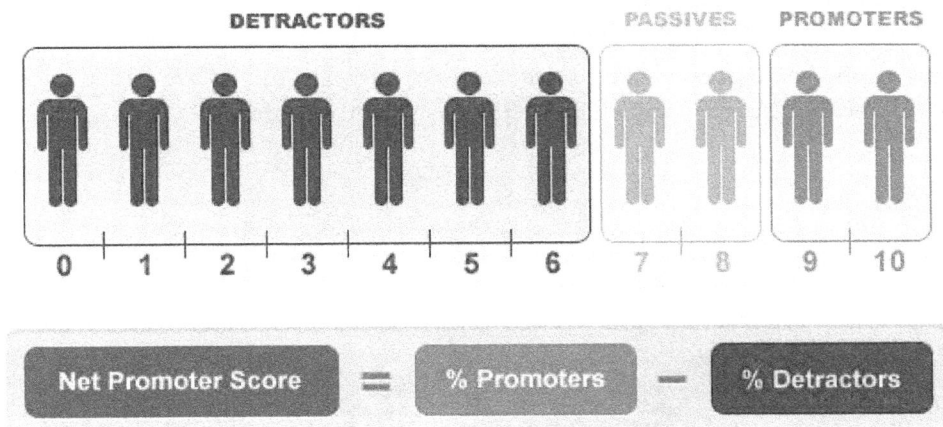

An example NPS questionnaire

To create the NPS score you take the percentage of people opting for 9 and 10, known as promoters and then deduct the total percentage of those who opted for 0 to 6, known as detractors.

So getting a high percentage is tough as few people go right to the extremes of any survey. Many will opt for 7 or 8 and these numbers are ignored. Get it?

Some companies ask a few more questions to make the most of the survey. The one I thought was the most powerful, asked 5 questions.

1. How likely are you to recommend us to friends, colleagues, associates?

2. Where can we improve?

3. Who's the biggest competitor to us?

4. How likely are you to recommend this competitor to friends, colleagues, associates?

5. What does this competitor do better than us?

Pretty smart eh? I love this package of five questions as it gives you real nuggets of information to improve and advance your service and customer care.

Next steps for NPS

Getting customers to do the survey is the hard part, you might want to outsource this part or use some of the companies online to help.

A final word of wisdom on customer service came recently from Seth Goden. I loved this, again so simple. Recruit nice people to give fine care to customers, then create processes that don't get in the way of them giving this naturally pleasant care.

Too many organisations create processes that prevent people giving this. Care and service are separate. Care is the people side; service is the processes and procedures.

Managing Your Day Using Tech

To CRM or not to CRM – that's the question

Most organisations I work with have some form of customer database or CRM – customer relationship management – system in place. If you do, then you should learn every aspect of it and use it to run your working life. Simple.

A good CRM will allow you to track every contact with a customer, what you said, what they said and the progress you made along your company's sales process. CRMs can be useful in curating data such as key performance indicators – KPIs and many of them have calendars and email management built in.

If you don't have a CRM system either buy one, lease one that's in the cloud such as Salesforce or use the latest version of Microsoft Outlook with the CRM add-on. Better still obtain Office 365 for yourself and your team, add the CRM bolt on and you're cooking on gas. If you're familiar with Outlook and the Office suite of products then your learning curve for Office 365 will be negligible. I'm going to show you how you can do this and finally get to grips with time and email management.

Office 365 is an Inside Salesperson's dream. Add on Dynamics CRM Online and you have the perfect intuitive solution. Everything you're doing in Office 365 will be logged and stored in this database. Your emails, tasks and appointments from Outlook can automatically be synchronised into the database. Your Word docs and Excel files can be stored there, too. Your conversations will be noted and saved. And not just for you – but for your whole company.

There's nothing worse for a customer than when he or she calls a company and they're treated like a stranger. That doesn't happen with a good CRM system. You and your employees are sharing all interactions with your community in the system. You have the system integrated with social media sites like Facebook and LinkedIn. You have emails, activities, notes, conversations and documents linked to every contact and account.

Let's get into Office 365.

Use the cloud

Office 365 sits in the cloud, in other words, it can be accessed from any device via the internet. It doesn't sit on an old fashioned hard-drive. This means you can pull data from any device, so set them all up first. Your phone, laptop, PC, tablet. Whenever an entry is made on any device, the database is updated in the cloud real time so anyone can see the information from their devices.

365 Contacts

The best feature here is the merge option where you can link your social media accounts to your contacts. So when you Link In with a new contact, their details automatically transfer into your contacts, with picture too.

If you get into the habit of photographing people you meet with your phone, incorporate this into the contact details. So when they phone your mobile, their name flashes up and photograph too. A picture brings back memories far quicker than text.

Emails from new contacts can be dragged into the contacts box and a contact entry is automatically made with all the details harvested from the email.

365 Calendar

Firstly set the options so your calendar looks like you want it to. Decide your working week, which may include Saturday, mine does. Sort out the default view for your calendar.

Now decide colours for differing items, here's my suggestion:

- Red – making money
- Blue – marketing activities
- Yellow – administration
- Green – self development
- Orange – personal activities.

You can then see at a glance whether you're being productive or not:

Microsoft provide an enterprise quality web meeting software platform called Skype for Business. It uses the Skype engine but it's not connected to your personal Skype. It allows you to run a web meeting with anyone or any group at the click of a button. Make sure you obtain this and link it into Office 365. It's far better than GoToWebinar and more cost effective too.

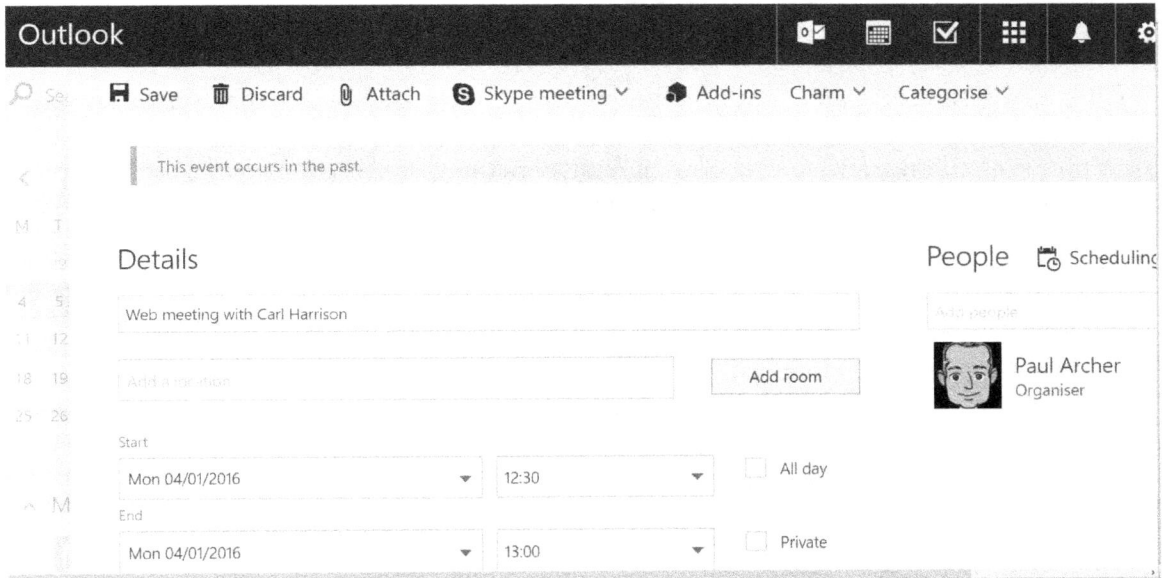

365 Tasks

Office 365 comes with a stable task management engine which is underused. Many people just list all their tasks into one giant "to do" list and this can be very bewildering.

There's a couple of ways you can convert your tasks into something more digestible. The first manner is to put dates on each task – start and end dates – so they appear at the bottom of your calendar for the relevant day. Handy if they must be done on that day.

I do it differently. I categorise each task so I can group them on my calendar. I believe I'm more productive when I'm doing similar tasks in clusters rather than free-wheeling.

Firstly, I'm crystal clear as to my objectives, supporting projects and goals I need to achieve. I'm sure you are too. With that in mind you should be choosy whether you add an item into tasks. You should only do this if it moves you forward in your objectives. If it does, it's known as a Tactical Next Action – a TNA.

I have TNAs for:

- TNA: Calls
- TNA: Online
- TNA: Do
- TNA: Write
- TNA: Someday maybe

The last one is true; I have 35 items in that category at the moment but none are deal breakers, but the first four are what my calendar carries most.

When a new task comes into your task list, put it in as unassigned – it will automatically find its way to the top, so when you do your task management, you can allocate a TNA to it. Use your phone to add tasks whenever you think of something or someone gives you a job to do. Don't rely on the brain to remember, it won't, but the phone will. The task will whiz into the cloud and synchronise across all devices.

365 Email

The foundation of all communications and one of your collection points. I'll talk about collection points shortly. But let's tame your email once and for all; I've known salespeople to drown in it. Here's how.

Before we go any further, turn off your email alert feature. This has to be one of the worst distractions known to the Inside Salesperson.

You are allowed to check email regularly for important items but it's best to do this every couple of hours – say 9am, 12 noon, 3pm and 5pm. But only to deal with urgent ones, leave the rest till later when you clear your inbox. For a quick reminder of urgent versus important you won't do worse than Stephen Covey's Time Management Grid. You can see below that he creates four boxes which determine whether a task should be done or delayed or even ignored.

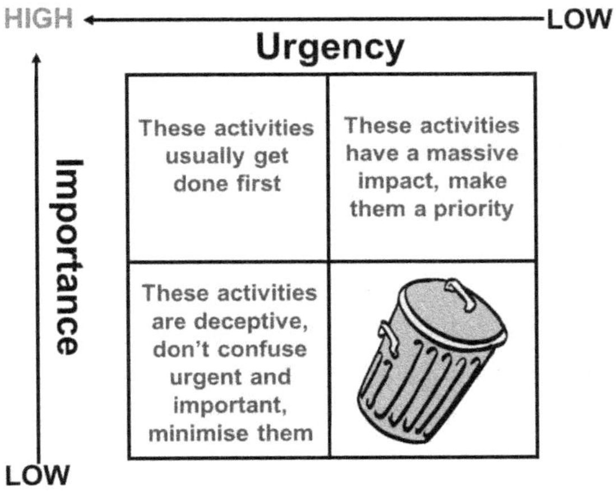

HIGH ←————————————LOW

Urgency

These activities usually get done first	These activities have a massive impact, make them a priority
These activities are deceptive, don't confuse urgent and important, minimise them	

Importance (vertical axis, left side)

LOW (bottom left)

If you really do need to keep tabs of urgent email as they come in, buy yourself a smartwatch and Bluetooth your inbox. I have a Microsoft Band which does this for me, it vibrates and you glance at the tiny screen without accessing email.

And you must clear your inbox every day. Here's how.

Choose a 60 minute window every day at some time, best before the close of play. Start with the first email. Can you handle it in less than 2 minutes? If so handle it. If it's going to take longer than 2 minutes, then put it into a task to be dealt with at another time. You can simply drag the email into the task area on Office 365 and it will automatically populate a task, which remains unassigned to be assigned an SNA later.

If it's something you don't want such as a subscription, see if you can unsubscribe. Be ruthless with these.

If it just needs filing somewhere, just drag it into the folder on your PC where it belongs.

Work your way through your emails in this manner and you will clear your inbox. And you must do this every day. Believe me, you'll feel good when you do.

Collection Points

This is my term for where information and communications come into your business. Have a quick think about what collection points you have. Here's mine when I first did this exercise:

- Texts
- Email
- Post
- In tray on my desk
- Desk

- Kitchen table
- Car dashboard
- Post-it notes on my computer screen
- Unassigned tasks on my phone
- Mobile voicemail
- Land-line voicemail
- Twitter direct messaging
- Facebook direct messaging
- Linked In direct messaging
- WhatsApp communications
- Ideas stored in my brain

The aim is to reduce them, I was ruthless because the more collection points you have, the more difficult it all becomes to keep in control and you'll soon be overwhelmed. Here's my culled list:

- Texts
- Office 365 Email
- Unassigned tasks for ideas etc.
- In tray on my desk for all paperwork including post
- Plastic folder in brief case for receipts etc.

Email is king for me, so I channel everything through to my email inbox and because I can access this on my phone, I don't miss a thing. All social media messages come through to email, eBay notifications everything. It does mean I have a full inbox every day but I do clear this each day.

Do all these things and you too will manage your time really effectively so you can concentrate on selling. I do.

Time Management Techniques

Clearing clutter

We're most productive when our energy levels are high but there are plenty of things that sap the energy. Periodically carry out an MOT by completing the following checklist.

1. Clean up your house, and or your office.
2. Clean up your car – inside and out. Get it valeted and serviced.
3. Throw away everything you don't use, haven't used for 6 months, or which is outdated. (Keep and file all business receipts)
4. File or throw away any unused papers.
5. Clean out all filing cabinets. Throw away unused materials.
6. Clean off the top of your desk. Throw away unused materials and any unneeded papers. File all papers you don't throw away.
7. File any past tax or business filings.
8. Get your accounts balanced. If self-employed get all financial statements (Profit & Loss, and Balance Sheet) up to date. Keep them up to date.
9. Pay all your bills or make arrangements and/or agreements as to when you will pay them. Keep those agreements.
10. Make a list of everyone who owes you money, or who has borrowed things. Write or call and ask for the money (or the thing borrowed), or cross the person off the list and decide it is complete.
11. Make a list of all the things you have started but not completed. Complete the list, or cross it off and decide not to do it.
12. Make a list of all the things you have started, are ongoing, and which are incomplete. Complete the list, or cross it off and decide not to do it.
13. Make a list of all the things, which have been going on a long time, but you have just not completed. Complete the list, or cross it off and decide not to do it.
14. Make a list of all the agreements you've made. Fulfil all past agreements. Renegotiate and make new agreements with any that you that can't fulfil.
15. Start taking care of your physical body – eat well, exercise well, sleep well, etc.

Curing procrastin'itis

Why we procrastinate:

- To escape an unpleasant or overwhelming task
- To excuse poor work
- To get someone else to do the job
- Fear that they won't be able to do the job
- Don't know where or how to start
- There won't be time to do the job perfectly
- Put easy, low priority jobs first

How to control procrastinating

- Admit you have been wasting time
- Decide work isn't necessarily unpleasant - adopt a positive attitude
- Separate your feelings about the job from your decision on what to do about it
- Recognise and acknowledge the futility of procrastination
- Decide to face unpleasant tasks square on
- Think through previous jobs - and recognise that fears of failure are usually unfounded. Use this to boost your confidence
- Decide to do the most unpleasant job of the day first
- Break the job down into small tasks - 15 minutes each day for a week instead of an entire half day
- Start anywhere, if starting is a problem
- Commit yourself by telling someone you're going to do the job
- Ask them to prompt you into action by a certain date and give yourself a reward when achieved
- Set your own deadline
- Reward yourself at stages through the job
- Analyse any 'slack time, when you typically receive fewer calls than usual (for example between 9 am. and 10 am). Arrange for someone to take calls during this period and return the favour for them as agreed. Ask the person taking the query to complete a standard form when taking your calls, so that you can deal with them later easily and effectively
- If one particular customer or department telephones you constantly with queries, turn the situation around by initiating the call to them. Schedule in proactive calls

at a guaranteed regular time to encourage them to save up their queries. This will result in a more effective personalised customer service

- If you are returning a call from a previous query, save up your calls and return them at an allotted time each day
- Be proactive. Analyse your calls so that you know why you are getting them and what can be done to stop them
- If a telephone call is going on too long and you need to get the call back on track, say the name of the person you are speaking to in order to regain control. Then use the opportunity to summarise the agreed actions with time-scales and such like
- If you receive calls querying letters which you (or your staff) have written, consider the possibility that the letters were unclear in the first place. Look into ways of improving them to reduce the number of queries generated
- If your screen indicates instantly whenever an e-mail arrives, discipline yourself to read your messages every couple of hours or look into the possibility of changing the screen to notify you every couple of hours

Time management rules

Know your time

Rule 1 Know where your time is going. You cannot control it until you know where it goes. A time log is an essential first step in finding where your time really does go.

Rule 2 Always plan your time. A plan for every day, every week, every month. Never start the day without a plan. Stand back from what needs to be done and the time available to do it. Block in time for every major task on your daily planner.

Rule 3 Allocate your time. Look at each task and decide on the best time to do it. Decide on what times of day can be under your own control and which times are at risk to unplanned interruptions and events. Do not start a job that you do not believe you can finish in the time available. Do not try to handle a job needing concentration at times of high vulnerability.

Save the little jobs for filling in your buffer time or for doing whilst waiting for someone to answer the phone - do not do them in quiet periods when you could be focusing your concentration and getting the best value out of your time.

Rule 4 Consolidate your time. Large chunks of contiguous time are far more valuable than small fragmented pieces. The time you manage directly is the most important time of all. Save it for those tasks that will benefit most from it. This time, your discretionary time, is precious. Guard it jealously and use it wisely. And above all, do not let the day-to-day immediacies squeeze it out of existence.

Set aside time each day for the difficult tasks and decide on a strategy for preserving your concentration during this time. Tell your colleagues what you are doing - get them to join in. Advise your staff and get them to adopt a similar programme so that you all work in harmony.

Know your purpose

Rule 5 Never lose sight of your goals. Every task and action you carry out should be measured in terms of its contribution towards achieving those goals.

Rule 6 Never lose sight of real priorities. The most important is rarely the most urgent. Never let the trees hide the wood. Maintain a constant overview of the whole job.

Rule 7 Let every task have a deadline. Tasks without deadlines get pushed back again and again. If it is worth doing put a date to it, if it is not worth doing cross it off the list.

Rule 8 Avoid the comfortable embrace of trivia. The trouble with trivial items is that they are so easy to do. They don't take long, they rarely need much mental effort, they don't call for major decisions - and because you can visibly see the pile diminishing as you work, you get that feeling of satisfaction of a job finished.

Rule 9 A job well done - is wasting time! Do not be a perfectionist, you cannot afford the time. Pareto's law applies perfectly to planning - 20% of effort achieves 80% of the results. Settle for achieving 80% if you can and free the remaining 20% of available effort.

Rule 10 Report by exception only. Wading through detailed reports looking for variances from the normal standard is a tedious and time-wasting process. It has become increasingly serious as computers take a tighter grip of a company, spitting out 4-inch thick printouts at every hapless manager. Refuse to read anything that hides important information in a sea of endless data. If everything is running according to plan you need not know about it.

Know your enemy

Rule 11 Recruit your colleagues in the war against time waste. Explain your problems and what you intend to do about them. Work on a joint strategy. Ask them to develop their own tactics.

Rule 12 Develop techniques to encourage callers to come to the point quickly - ask whether the call will take long (implying that time is short or that you have a visitor with you).

Rule 13 Do your visitors a favour - help them get to the point. Before they launch off into their reasons for being in your office, ask them how long they will be, it helps to focus their mind on the time they are taking and highlights the fact that your time is short. If they have a lot to tell you, ask them to write to you in advance of their visit so that you can brief yourself before they arrive.

Rule 14 Be courteous to your colleagues - go to them! Colleagues who like to "just drop in" (and especially those that tend to stay once they are settled comfortably into your office) need special treatment. A favourite trick is to make a habit of going to their office - then you can choose to leave when you like.

Rule 15 Subordinates need time management techniques too. Get them to work on their own programme. Encourage them to make their own decisions. Get them to group their questions and problems together and bring them to you in batches at pre-arranged times. Brief them on your own time management programme and have the whole department work in harmony with it.

Rule 16 Making the most of meetings. More time is wasted more often by more people in more companies through meetings than through any other means. For example, there is nothing more wasteful of executives' time than six people standing about waiting to start a meeting because one person is late.

Does every meeting have an agenda? Does everybody have all necessary information in advance? Remember that the effectiveness of meetings tends to be inversely proportional to the number of people attending them. Re-time your meetings to start at 11.00 or 4.30, to provide an incentive to keep on time.

Know yourself

Rule 17 Do unto others. Ask yourself whether you waste other people's time. Do you talk too much? Are you ever late for meetings? Do you just "drop in" on colleagues.

Rule 18 Handle it at once. Get out of the habit of "putting it aside until later". When the post arrives, avoid scanning it to see if there is anything interesting in the pile. Take the first one off the top of the pile and deal with it. Do not put it down until you have decided on some specific action. If it is a lengthy document and you expect to refer to it again later, use a highlighter pen to pick out the essential points for fast scanning. You should have no use for a "procrastination file".

Rule 19 Handle it by the shortest route. Constantly ask yourself "is there a quicker way?" Remember Pareto's law.

Rule 20 Don't do it! Try saying to yourself - "What would happen if this were not done?" Is it really essential? Is it being done simply because it has always been done? What would be the effect if it were not done?

Rule 21 Delegate! Delegate! Delegate! Delegation is like driving - nobody would ever admit to being a bad driver and similarly, no manager would admit to being a bad delegator. The problem is the way different managers perceive the meaning of the word.

Hand out the whole job, along with the responsibility and authority for seeing it through. But only after having first decided on the capabilities of the person involved, having described the scope of the job in detail, the results to be achieved, any constraints that exist and the deadline. Then leave that person alone to get on with it.

Rule 22 If it happens more than once - make it a routine. A task always takes longer to do the first time. Anything that occurs more than once should have a routine established for it. It then needs no further thought and planning, can be delegated and will flow with the rest of the workload. Keep checklists of all these jobs as a reminder of what you have established.

Rule 23 Review your desk driving skills. Make a habit of working with a clear desk. You can only work on one job at a time, everything else on your desk is simply a distraction. Prevent people from just dropping papers onto the top of your desk by having a clearly marked "in tray" - and reassure people that you are using it by making a point of emptying it regularly.

Rule 24 Never write if you can phone. It saves your time, it saves money and it is friendlier. Group the calls together and have minor tasks to hand whilst you are waiting for people to answer. Very late in the day is a good time to make these calls, people are less inclined to chat.

Rule 25 Learn not to read everything. Only read essentials. Make a habit of being selective. Delegate inessential reading - ask people to read it and let you know if it should contain anything important. Consider a course on faster reading - it could save many hours every week.

Rule 26 Learn to say "no". The hardest skill of all. It will sometimes need every ounce of your diplomacy and at other times, every ounce of your courage. However, there is no doubt that successful executives are those who have learnt to concentrate their effort on what is important. "Nice" people who try to oblige are often popular - but they pay a price. Saying "no" may not win you many friends at the time, but it can win respect when handled well.

109 time management tips

1. Ask for shorter or better-structured reports.
2. Start the day with unpleasant tasks you've been putting off.
3. Plan time to talk with subordinates individually.
4. Cut out activities that would not be missed.
5. Delegate attendance at meetings.
6. Invest more time in training your staff.
7. Build into your plans an allowance for unplanned time.
8. Let people know if they waste your time.
9. Delegate travelling, visits.
10. Have shorter meetings.

11. Have stand-up meetings.
12. Shorten communication routes – improve information systems.
13. Identify recurrent crises and make them routine.
14. Find somewhere inaccessible to work on important things.
15. Before interrupting someone, think whether it is really necessary.
16. Learn to say no.
17. Consolidate frequent short contacts with an individual into a regular meeting.
18. Avoid distractions - don't sit where you can gaze out of a window.
19. Tidy your desk.
20. Improve storage and filing systems.
21. Cut the joking and get down to business.
22. Accept that few tasks can be done to perfection.
23. Change the office layout; turn your desk around, so that you are not inviting interruptions.
24. Have fewer meetings.
25. Identify time wasters and root them out.
26. Learn rapid reading techniques.
27. Cut down on reading.
28. Consolidate your time into worthwhile chunks.
29. Link everything you do to the job's results.
30. Stop analysing, do something to improve.
31. Improve meetings - chairmanship, agenda, and discipline.
32. Ask your staff how you waste their time.
33. Let people know that your closed door means, "interrupt only if urgent".
34. Get rid of visitors as soon as the business is done.
35. Handle each piece of paper only once.
36. Make more use of standard letters and memos.
37. Check up on people less.
38. Accept uncertainty – take a few risks.
39. Don't get obsessed with details.
40. Work at home for an hour and come in later.
41. Finish what you start.
42. Keep a time log regularly to monitor improvement.
43. Carry with you a notebook, including a list of things to do.
44. Change your lunch-hour to get some time alone.
45. Press for a system of flexible working hours.

46.   Leave early and work at home.

47.   When you leave your office, let someone know where you are going and for how long.

48.   Use your PA more to screen interruptions.

49.   Ask to be dropped from some subscription lists.

50.   Delegate some reading - trust people to tell you if there is something you should see.

51.   Keep physically fit to be alert and make the best use of your time.

52.   Get all socialising done in coffee/lunch/tea breaks.

53.   Get a coffee machine and manage without a break.

54.   Live nearer the job.

55.   Work longer hours.

56.   Avoid people who share your outside interests.

57.   Rank your tasks for the day or week as high, medium or low priority.

58.   Share your problems and ideas with a colleague.

59.   Screen your calls before you answer.

60.   Find out how new technology can help you save time.

61.   Use tea breaks systematically for communication with staff and colleagues.

62.   Identify tasks that are related, especially those concerning the same people, and tackle them together.

63.   Start meetings mid-afternoon.

64.   To improve self-discipline, commit yourself by voluntarily making promises to other people.

65.   Negotiate time quality/bargains with people who want your services.

66.   Take up relaxation, yoga or meditation exercises.

67.   Draw up a "who-can-do-what" matrix of staff abilities, as an aid to planning delegation.

68.   If you are subject to Parkinson's Law, deliberately put off starting a task until the last possible moment.

69.   Lock the door.

70.   Eat better food.

71.   Make greater use of informal communication channels.

72.   Use a wall-chart to plan the year.

73.   Practise being more assertive, to answer back people who take advantage of your good nature.

74.   At the start of a meeting, always ask what time it is expected to finish.

75. Before starting new task, remind yourself you have options: what other tasks could you do instead?
76. Set yourself deadlines and treat them as unbreakable.
77. For a big job, set intermediate deadlines.
78. Plan time for domestic, social and personal needs.
79. Stop solving all your subordinates' problems for them: encourage them to solve their own.
80. Book appointments for meetings with yourself.
81. Set aside one hour a day when you do not accept interruptions, and let your staff and colleagues know.
82. Recognise that a task's urgency is nothing to do with its importance.
83. If you get bored after an hour or two on the same task, switch to something else.
84. Before spending a lot of time on a decision, ask what would be the cost of getting it wrong.
85. Plan time for self-development activities.
86. At the end of the day, list the tasks you didn't get around to doing: assess their importance to the job's key areas.
87. Set your digital watch to bleep on the hour, reminding yourself and others how time is getting on.
88. Mute the phone.
89. Promise yourself a brief "treat" (something you enjoy doing, whether work or not), for when you have finished a task you are tempted to put off.
90. Make a special point of always being punctual for appointments.
91. Start meetings on time, even if not all members have arrived.
92. Don't offer visitors coffee.
93. Have a clock in the office.
94. Sit visitors on uncomfortable chairs.
95. Get the PA to interrupt meetings after a given time.
96. Before accepting a phone call, find out who and what it's about.
97. Keep staff fully briefed so they can solve problems.
98. Circulate fuller information before meetings.
99. Let staff know you expect them to have thought of options before coming to you with problems.
100. When necessary, hang a "do not disturb" sign on the door.
101. Get double-glazing to reduce distraction by noise.

102.   If there is information that you need to refer to often (e.g., prices, rates, phone numbers), keep it pinned on the wall by your desk rather than hidden in files and drawers.

103.   Confront the boss and demand to know the objectives and priorities.

104.   Ensure all staff are pulling their weight.

105.   Hire a hotel's meeting room for long, uninterrupted meetings.

106.   Arrange with a colleague that one of you will take all the phone calls while the other is working on something important.

107.   Learn to use the "qwerty" keyboard properly, using the right fingers, so your writing can keep pace with your thinking.

108.   Ensure the organisation structure is suitable for getting the work done.

109.   Dictate correspondence in a daily batch.

Choosing Your Mood

It's your call

Working on the telephone, selling things or advising or just taking calls from people…is extremely hazardous to your health and wellbeing.

Seriously it is.

But you can also be very hazardous to your customers or people you talk to purely by the mood you bring into work with you.

Picture this. Brian has had a terrible night – he had an argument with his partner, and his middle son was very poorly during the night and was up and down like a yo-yo causing poor Brian to wake up several times to see to him.

He missed the bus on his way to work. It was raining cats and dogs.

He arrived at work, soaked to the skin, and was told by his supervisor that a complaint has been lodged against him. And his second call of the day was from a customer who was in an even worse mood than Brian. What sort of frame of mind do you think Brian will be in? Pretty dire I'm sure.

The key here is that we can all choose our mood, but circumstances influence this during the day. We all need strategies to help us deal with mood swings and we need to adopt these to help us choose our mood.

What is the Inner Game?

I wanted to sub title this book "At last some new ideas on handling the Inner Game" but thought this was a little condescending to all the books previously published on the subject, some of them are really good.

However you will get some new ideas here I promise you.

The Inner Game is a term taken from sports psychology to mean the workings of the athlete's mind and how this affects their performance.

It's widely known and accepted that all performers, whether athletes or sales people, are influenced by what goes on in their heads.

The inner voice, the internal motivation, the ups and downs of life, the drive, the direction, the attitude…are all created and influenced by the ability of the salesperson to control the Inner Game.

9 attitudes of top performing salespeople

Attitude rules OK!

It's often been said that salespeople need three components to thrive – knowledge, skills and attitude. We're all guilty of focusing far too much time and energy on the first two – knowledge and skills, neglecting the pursuit of the right attitudes. All three oil the gears of a top performing salesperson, but attitude is the highest grade oil.

Attitude is the most important attribute of top performing salespeople, without doubt but the wrong attitude can be heavily damaging.

Here are 9 attitudes that all top performing salespeople share.

Determination

Determined sales people get what they want and they refuse to accept defeat. Determination was made famous by Thomas Edison – the inventor of the light bulb and many other creations. Edison was celebrated for making thousands of attempts before achieving success. He was quoted "When I have fully decided that a result is worth getting I go ahead with it and make trial after trial until it comes."

Assertiveness

Assertiveness in a salesperson means being proactive and not reacting to events, having a plan and driving towards this. Assertive salespeople make their presence felt and thrive on competition, ultimately producing results.

Responsibility

Motivated salespeople take responsibility for everything – their own business, their results, their successes, their failures. They accept responsibility for errors, no blame and no excuses – they see their mistakes and correct them moving forward. They also accept success and know how to celebrate and bottle it.

Inner strength

Inner strength means to be able to recover from setbacks, knock downs and other events that cause most people to stall. "What's the worst that can happen?" is a question they might ask themselves as they quickly recover, shake off the dust and pull themselves together. Inner strength is all about handling the self dialogue that dominates all salespeople, the nagging voice that can put you down. Motivated high performers learn to cope with these voices and channel them towards ambition, quickly putting the past behind them.

Inner desire

Top performers have an innate inner desire to achieve their goals. Firstly they set goals, turning them into compelling outcomes with strategic next actions littering their direction. Moving on their goals, they generate their own energy. Either gaining motivation from external sources or, more commonly from within themselves – their internal burner. Many salespeople adopt mental rehearsal techniques taken from sports psychology, and this allows them to practice the future before it happens, giving them further inner desire to win.

Self confidence

Top performing salespeople have confidence in their own abilities, they never doubt themselves. However they are not arrogant or obnoxious, just confident – there's a fine line and they don't cross it. They just know they are capable of achieving their goals.

Trust

Top performing salespeople ooze trust. In others – particularly their teams that support them. They communicate well with their teams, often motivational and encouraging to others. They are good delegators to their support teams and use them appropriately.

Influencers

Top performers have a range of influencing styles that they can flex to suit the occasion. Both pull and push style influencing is used. They like to influence, find it easy and take control of situations which require control.

Coachability

Salespeople that reach the top and remain so, enjoy and relish coaching from a sales manager. They are good at being coached, are willing and receptive to the words of a quality coach. They know how to accept feedback, quickly eliminating criticism in their minds as constructive guidance. They either accept or reject the feedback and then act on it quickly and decisively…and move forward. They don't dwell on it. Today is another day and my goals drive me forward.

What makes good performance?

We mustn't miss out on the impact of good skills and solid knowledge in promoting performance. These three attributes make up the salesperson's worth and can be compared to the gears of a motor, each one moving the other.

Only recently, many pundits thought skills and knowledge were the major influencer, but more and more research is conclusively proving that the principal one is attitude.

In fact, recent research from the States shows attitude to have a 50% impact on the salesperson's performance.

Call reluctantitis

One of the biggest barriers to making appointment calls is your own Inner Game.

Those little voices in your head, which keep saying "Don't call now, it's lunchtime", or "They won't want to talk to me anyway", "I'll call after lunch". "It's too late to call."

The fear of rejection or call reluctance is endemic and can cause a fatal flaw in the whole process, so let's get the Inner Game sorted first.

If you ever suffer from Call Reluctantitis, then answer these questions:

```
┌──────────────────┐     ┌──────────────────┐     ┌──────────────────┐
│    Have you      │     │ Do you believe in│     │ Do you know the  │
│  researched the  │ ──▶ │  your solutions? │ ──▶ │  business of the │
│    industry?     │     │                  │     │  person you're   │
│                  │     │                  │     │     calling?     │
└──────────────────┘     └──────────────────┘     └──────────────────┘
                                                           │
                                                           ▼
┌──────────────────┐     ┌──────────────────┐     ┌──────────────────┐
│ Can you definitely│    │  Are you aware of│     │  Are you aware of│
│ look at solving his│◀─ │   the value you  │ ◀── │ the trigger events?│
│    problems?     │     │     provide?     │     │                  │
└──────────────────┘     └──────────────────┘     └──────────────────┘
         │
         ▼
┌──────────────────┐     ┌──────────────────┐
│ Can you reel off the│  │ Do you believe in│
│ value you've already│─▶│   yourself, your │
│ provided to existing│  │  company and the │
│     clients?     │     │ value you provide?│
└──────────────────┘     └──────────────────┘
```

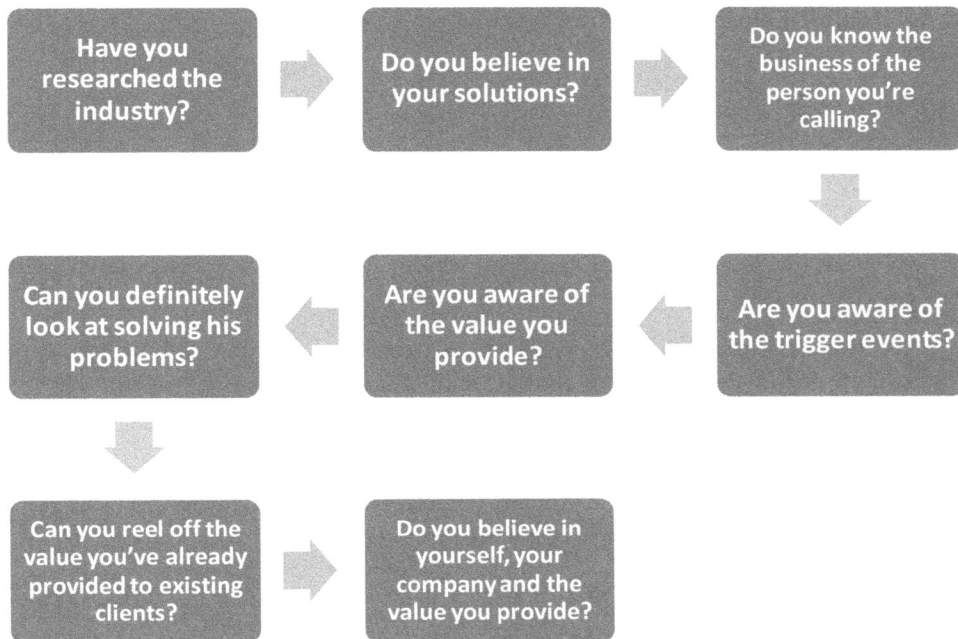

Answering "yes" to these questions ought to convince your Inner Game to make that call and give you soaring self confidence and esteem.

Overcoming call reluctance

A few people wrote to me just before Christmas asking for help. Both were struggling to get in front of new prospects to sell their services and products. Both had excellent propositions but found call reluctance to be a problem and prospects' unwillingness to speak with them, preferring to "weather the storm" and batten down the hatches.

Have you experienced this as well?

I think we all have to some degree and unless you've had your head in the sand, you'll recognise that we are going through a downturn. Now I don't sign up for the "Business is better that it's ever been, I'm busier than ever, what recession?" brigade; these people seem to be just massaging their egos when they print this stuff.

The plain fact is - we have to prospect more than ever before. Working harder and smarter at getting to speak with new customers, will help us succeed in this economy.

I think we've all got the skills but maybe haven't had to use them so much over the last five to six years since there's been plenty of business to go around.

So now's the time to smarten up our prospecting tools, or client acquisition tools as this is now known as.

Some quick reminders:

- Examine your product and service and be crystal clear as to what problem it solves. Problems in recessions are all about saving costs and increasing revenue, getting invoices paid on time, preventing suppliers going bust and such like. Try to think like your customers and be totally clear as to what problems your product solves.

- What is your customer segment? Be as precise as you can as to which type of customer has the problems that your product or service solves and then focus on these customers.

- Decide on your marketing to reach these customers. There are many routes to market that you can choose but the quickest and most decisive is still telephoning them to make an appointment to see them.

- Get over any call reluctance.

- Dedicate specific blocks of time in your diary to make calls to prospects.

- Aim simply for a face to face appointment, nothing else. Don't get into conversations, send out literature etc. These never work, although we think they do at the time, are easy to do, quite gratifying but divert your attention to the job of making appointments.

- Be up front with your prospect on the phone about the problem that your product solves and ask for an appointment.

- Don't ask "If it's convenient to call", you'll lose sales if you do this. Instead say "If it's convenient to speak right now, I'd like to…" Subtle difference. And if you feel brave enough, don't even ask, just launch into your opening.

- Learn how to politely persevere on objections twice and then leave the prospect alone. Keep coming back to the objective of asking for an appointment.

- Sticky tape the phone to your wrist and don't put it down. Use the 60 second rule. This ensures you get onto the next call within 60 seconds, no longer.

- Spend a maximum of 60 minutes making appointment calls.

- Reward yourself when you're done as making appointments is stressful, there's no way around it. Yes, alpha male macho types will tell you they enjoy it but you look at the burnout rate of call centre direct sales people. It's hard, full of rejection and people saying no, occasional rudeness and extremely easy to put off to do another job.

We all need more prospects right now and making appointments via phone is the quickest and most effective method of doing so. Dig out all those customers that have connections to your company, old names and phone numbers. Those people who you never had the time to contact. Maybe buy some lists or leads and start to make those calls with the specific intention of making an appointment.

10 Strategies to Coach Call Centre Salespeople

Over the last three months, I've been working closely with a major insurance company helping their telephone handlers to upskill themselves in their soft skills. The aim is to improve the experience the customer gets when they make a call to the company.

The type of customer was irrelevant, they could be internal from another department or external from a paying customer or insurance broker and the reason for their call didn't matter either.

My input was coaching the handlers live on the job and to work with them to make them better at what they did. Being an expert from outside the company really helped me to give everyone some real benefit. Even those who had been on the phones for many years, were receptive and learnt a few things they could do differently to improve their customer experience.

This article will share with you 10 of my strategies and some of the tips that I used during my coaching, that you might want to use yourself when coaching or pass on to your team leaders or in-company coaches.

Ditch classic coaching strategies

I'm sorry to say but classic coaching doesn't always work in a fast paced call centre environment. By classic coaching I mean mainly the structures quoted in books. The style is different though and still works well, so carry on asking questions such as:

- "How did it go?"
- "What did you do well?"
- "How could you do that differently?"

These always work in classic coaching and should be used early on, however don't keep using them after each observed call as you'll turn into a parrot, repeating yourself time and again. You see in a typical 45 minutes stint, you'll get to feedback on about 7 – 9 calls and if you keep asking "how did it go?" after each one, they'll soon start just ignoring you.

Models such as GROW and PESOS don't work, it's the wrong environment. No, instead we need to focus on a feedback model.

Sell the session

Far too many call handlers had been coached before with the sole intention of having their style observed and compared against a checklist of what good looks like. Now don't get me wrong, this is a vital management tool or indicator and long may it live on. But it's not coaching and shouldn't be called it. The first thing I wanted to do with my people was remove this connection that they all had in their mind and do this in the first moments of meeting them. I used words such as:

"Now before we start let me show you how this coaching is going to be different and valuable for you. As an external communications expert, I'm able to work with you now by listening in to your calls and giving you expert feedback on what you are doing really well and suggest possible areas that you can do differently to make you even better. I'm not going to checklist you and mark you, that's so not what this is all about – I'm here to work with you and make you even better than you are right now."

I like to use the phrase "I want to work with you" it sounds much better than coaching, which I'm afraid, many people still connect with training or watching closely over them.

Build a rapport quickly

In any one to one, eye ball to eye ball, belly button to belly button interaction, we simply must build a rapport with people. Some of the unique things I do in this situation really help me to get on their side and lighten them. You want them to be relaxed otherwise the call won't work; they'll perform differently because they feel under pressure.

I make sure I'm sitting on their favourite side, out of earshot with other handlers (although this is tricky sometimes). I ask them which side they would like me to sit on. I then ensure my eye level is the same as theirs by lowering and raising the seat. I don't want to be looking down on them. Eye contact is important so I match the amount of eye contact they give me. Small talk is useful but usually the hectic nature of the call environment limits this.

I think it's important to model the skills you want them to use such as voice matching. This should be second nature to me, so naturally I voice match them. Finally get them talking freely about themselves and their job – what they enjoy, what challenges they have, maybe just chatting about who they are and what gets them up in the morning. But quickly get down to the first call.

Have a structure

Structure is imperative to call handlers and the tip I want to give you here is to outline this for them at the outset and continue to signpost it throughout the coaching session. Signposting is a key ingredient for them when dealing with customers on the phone so we need to signpost them during the coaching session. Remember, no surprises.

"After our initial chat we'll listen to two calls without stopping, then I'd like you to break off for a moment whilst we have some feedback. Then we can go back on a call and if you could break off after each one, we'll have a brief feedback before going onto the next call. In about 45 minutes we'll then wrap up and take your thoughts. Sound OK?"

Are they an "A" grade student?

I call this a pre-brief. Before the first call comes in, set the scene by asking them what they would want you to specifically listen out for and give them feedback on. This often comes as a surprise to them as previous coaching involves going straight into a call. So be prepared to probe on this area as you'll get the "I dunno" answer. Relate it to some training that might have occurred beforehand or maybe to some form of team leader feedback.

Do you remember at school when you turned in your homework and received the results? Did you constantly get As or were you more of a B student or C possibly – with the note from teacher saying "room for improvement"?

Kind of brings back a memory doesn't it, but this can be extremely useful when pre-briefing. If you get little information from them after asking the question, it's worth asking them to grade their ability in handling calls. You could use the B+ format or marks out of ten – it doesn't matter.

"So if you were to grade your average call from 1 to 10, where would you place yourself?"

"Urrr, I guess 7 or 8."

"That's great. Out of interest, what would a 10 out of 10 call look like?"

"For you to get a perfect 10, what would you want to do differently?"

This works so it's worth giving it a go.

Give dollops of praise

This morning my car was covered in ice so I popped out 10 minutes early to run the engine and de ice and de-mist it. I ran the engine for about 5 minutes so when I climbed in, the car was lovely and toasty and the engine humming, unlike me!

Just like a car on a very frosty morning, my people needed warming up too and the best way I've found to do this, is to listen to one or two calls to start with and point out to them the positive aspects that I noticed. I've found the most effective way to do this is to say what you heard them do or say, explain why this is good and the positive impact it had on the customer. For example, "I really do like the way your voice sounds chirpy and enthusiastic, you're able to do this because you have a good vocal range and can stretch your voice to maximum effect. The customer feels as though you are very human and genuinely interested in them. Well done."

Rather better than "You have a good voice".

Even the most hardened and experienced call handler will revel in this and it is particularly important for the newer handler who is often a little nervous. The next call you listen to will be far more natural and an indication as to how they normally work.

Look away

Once I'm hooked up with the phone listening device, I like to look away from the call handler and their computer screen as you can easily get caught up in the detail of the call, and irrelevant observations.

It's the verbal and vocal aspects we want to pick up on. I want to listen to the voices of both people; I want to sense the customer and how they are feeling. How do they react to what's being said, their tone of voice, their pace? That way I can look for matching and leading, and emotions rather than the content and subject of the call.

Use "different", not "wrong"

This is so simple yet so powerful. I've overheard many coaches giving feedback focused on what the person is doing wrong. Now this is fine as making the person aware of this is a major purpose of the coaching session. I prefer to be more practical and suggest something they should do differently which overcomes the weak area.

This is much more motivational and practical.

For example, if they are talking too fast and the customer can't understand them I would say something like:

"I noticed the customer asked you to repeat what you were saying a couple of times. Something you could do differently is to add a bit more of a gap between your sentences. If you were to do this, the customer would understand your question first time and this would save you time."

Rather than, "I noticed the customer asked you to repeat what you were saying, this is because you were speaking too quickly."

Give sandwich feedback

It's as old as them there hills. Sometimes called burger feedback aka the McDonalds Model or just sandwich feedback. The one that works for me is this:

- Tell them what they did well and the impact. Be genuine.

- Here's what you could do differently and the impact it would have. Just one thing and it must be the priority.

- Your overall impression of the call which needs to be positive and upbeat.

It's three parts and can be done quickly and efficiently. Don't get into longwinded discussion, if they don't agree with you, that's just fine. Get over it and move on, and next time give some evidence as to why doing it differently next time would make a difference.

Work with priorities

The longest time you'll want to work with someone is 1 hour – I normally work for about 45 minutes. This gives you time to listen to plenty of calls and give feedback.

However we can't cover every aspect and give lots of varying feedback. Not only would this be nigh on impossible in the timeframe, but frankly quite de-motivating if there are just too many points discussed.

So instead focus on just one or two main priority points of feedback that you can spot early on. Priority points, once taken care of, have a knock on effect on other areas and it's this feedback we want to give. Then give them a chance to change on the next call and feel the difference it makes and then to try this new angle a few times during your coaching. Not only is this good training practise i.e. repetition is the mother of all skill, but it's very motivating when you've given some feedback, they've adopted it and are getting better results.

These are my secrets to successfully coaching call handlers in a live company environment, shared freely to help us all improve the effectiveness and receptiveness of quality coaching. Good luck and good coaching.

No Nonsense Inside Sales

20 Call Centre Coaching Tips

To achieve a culture of regular coaching being the way we work around here, her are 20 tips to help you in your busy call centre environment:

1. Have a policy of shutting down email from 10am for all coaches, that way you can swarm over your people and conduct side by side coaching, which is what you should be doing.

2. Be clear on the coaching that will work for individual agents. You can use learning styles. For example, activist agents will respond well to side by side coaching as they are more than likely to come out with quick actions and responses. Pragmatists will like this too. Reflector agents will cringe with the rapidity of the side by side so will prefer the pre-recorded playback sessions in privacy so they can think through how they can improve. Theorist types will also like this, but will want to have access to the calls beforehand. You could get them to choose their best and perceived worst one to analyse, otherwise ensure you use intelligent software to choose the calls for you. Don't spend time trawling through the whole lot, use technology to help you here.

3. Rather than just one agent listening to their pre-recorded calls, encourage a small group to listen to them and all to add comments and share best practice. Allow each agent to complete your best practice checklist as they listen to the calls. Then you facilitate an empowering session.

4. Have a "Caught you doing something great" emblem to plant on the desktop. One client of mine bought "Wow" lollypops – the large versions – and gave one to an agent when they did something wow.

5. Have a lucky dip bin for great performances. Inside the bin will be booby prizes as well or ones requiring a forfeit.

6. When doing side by side coaching, keep the feedback sharpish and precise. Use the session to work on a theme or encourage your agent to suggest a theme before the session starts.

7. Feedback is mostly needed with side by side coaching. Don't do too much of the "How would you do that differently?", you can leave that for your recorded call coachings.

8. Get a routine going with your agents. Allow them to expect lots of coaching from you. Alternate it with side by side coaching followed a few days later with some

recorded coaching, some engagement Q&A type coaching and then back to some side by side. Get a routine going.

9.   Skills development is a fine outcome of coaching but use your side by side coaching to get an appreciation of the non-skill based performance inhibitors. Try to understand the real challenges they're under, that'll build empathy.

10.   In your recorded call coaching sessions, allow your agent to run the call best practice checklist themselves on their actual call before giving you feedback.

11.   If you're dealing with a low performer, attempt to pick more than a couple of calls to analyse and coach on, the more the better.

12.   After every coaching session you must have the magical three outcomes. WHY is the acronym – what, how and you. Your agent should know *what* they need to do, *how* they can get there and what *you* and the business can do to support them. If they don't know these, then you'll have to spend time GROW-ing them.

13.   Use the GROW model by all means, but be aware that it was never designed for a call centre environment. It was originally designed for tennis players and athletes to help them achieve their goals. A tip is to start the GROW model at R = reality, by providing feedback or self-discovered feedback on performance. That way your agent is aware of their current performance where a goal can evolve to improve it.

14.   Always, always, always do coaching after any form of assessment. Even if it's billed as a Q&A type observation, empower these people to do a little bit of coaching afterwards. Never leave observation and assessment in isolation otherwise it'll get a "police" type reputation.

15.   Ask agents what kind of coaching and development they would like. The type, the duration, how else can you support their skills and development. Naturally your coaching outcomes must be beneficial for the agents otherwise they just might say "none please".

16.   Have best practice meetings for 5 minutes each morning and evening to share best practices and great performances. Stand up and let different agents run them for you.

17.   Get your call recording software to burn calls onto a CD or SD Card, as many as will fit on, and get in the habit of listening to these on your way home or whilst in the gym. The habit of listening to lots of calls will help you to determine how your agents are doing and what ways they can improve.

18.   Have your call best practice checklist which contains the process plus all the soft areas needed to perform a great call. Also have your playbook which holds every technique, strategy and method which brings the call to life. Like a best practice

bible. This would need to be added to continually from observations and agents' new ideas.

19. Have a No PC day once a week so you get to surge over your agents all day.

20. Have a balanced scorecard approach for your metrics and measures. Learn to distinguish between lead and lag. Lead measures are those that'll help you judge how the agent is doing and get in some coaching to improve things. Lag measures are after the event, and although coaching may help, the event has happened. A Balanced Scorecard approach could use 4 measures:

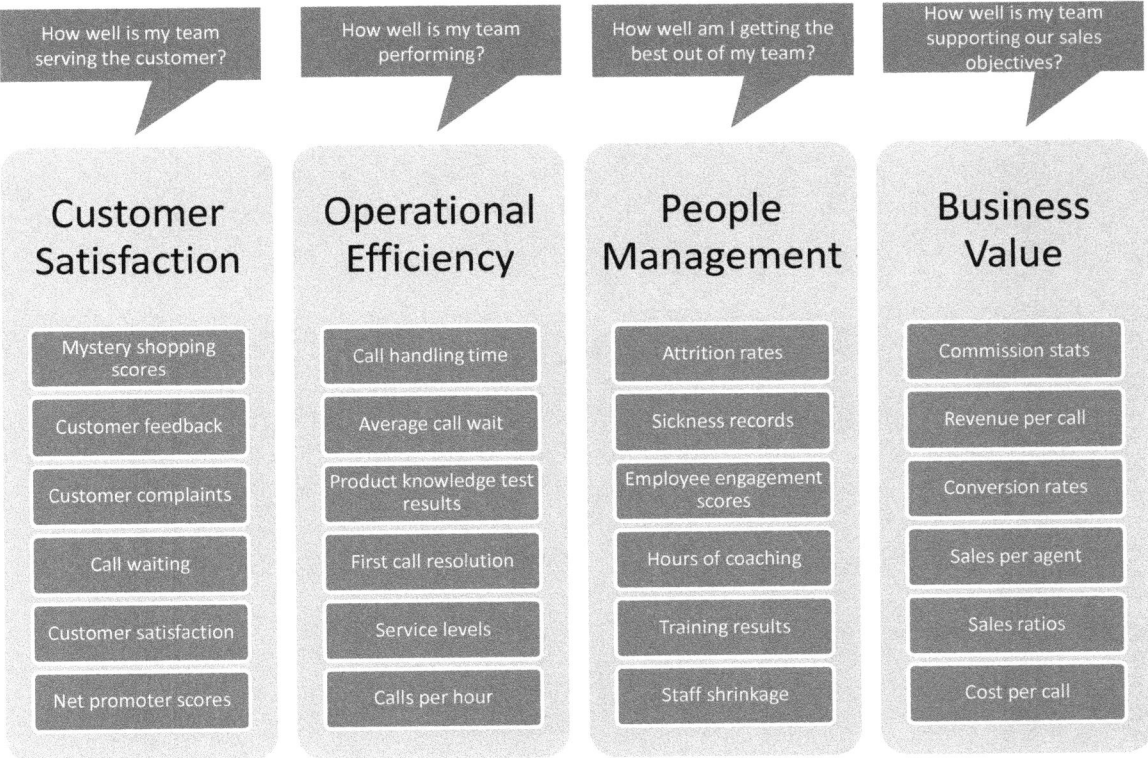

How well is my team serving the customer?	How well is my team performing?	How well am I getting the best out of my team?	How well is my team supporting our sales objectives?
Customer Satisfaction	**Operational Efficiency**	**People Management**	**Business Value**
Mystery shopping scores	Call handling time	Attrition rates	Commission stats
Customer feedback	Average call wait	Sickness records	Revenue per call
Customer complaints	Product knowledge test results	Employee engagement scores	Conversion rates
Call waiting	First call resolution	Hours of coaching	Sales per agent
Customer satisfaction	Service levels	Training results	Sales ratios
Net promoter scores	Calls per hour	Staff shrinkage	Cost per call

Inside Sales Coaching and Learning Styles

Learning styles and coaching

We're all very familiar with Honey and Mumford's Learning Styles piece of work from the 1980s which describes the four varying styles of learning that we all have. My preferred style is a reflector since I like to look back on my learning events, take my time when learning, think things through, listen to others and I hate being dropped in at the deep end.

Others might prefer an activist style where being dropped in from a thousand feet would suit them, happy to learn from mistakes, can easily see what their mistakes have been and can figure out an alternative way in mini seconds. They just seem to want workshops to soar at a hundred miles per hour.

You might prefer a theorist style with a desire to look at all the detail and background to the training topic and to see where theories and models can benefit your learnings.

Or finally the pragmatist who, by now, has got bored with this piece because they don't see the benefits and how it can help them.

Have you ever used these learning styles to help you maximise your phone based sales coaching? You may not have thought about it but it makes perfect sense.

Most phone sales centres or call centres or Inside Sales Operations as our friends across the Pond call them, use a variety of coaching interventions. These are:

1. Live side by side coaching in the call centre

2. Recorded call coaching in privacy

3. 1to1 coaching with metrics and KPIs

4. Group listening sessions followed by facilitated group discussion on best practice

If you have a choice which one you use with your phone salespeople, then choose the one that fits their learning style.

Side by side coaching

For activists – definitely go for live side by side coaching. Here's some tips to make this coaching better for them:

- Decide on a theme to work on during the side by sides and listen out for this area during your observations.

- Ask your agent for their preferred theme to focus on.

- Focus mostly on feedback and keep it snappy, then ask them what they can do differently.

- Use GROW but start on reality by giving them feedback on the reality that you just observed, then launch straight into options, giving them a chance to comment.

- Keep the feedback to around 2 minutes, then get on the next call.

- The beauty of live side by side is that you get to see the actual challenges they're facing which are non-skill based, normally system or process, so empathise with them and take some action to improve these.

Recorded feedback sessions

For reflectors – give them more private recorded call coaching sessions. Here's some tips to help you here:

- Give them slightly longer with the "How well did you do?" question, look away a little more, give them space to think.

- Let your agent choose the calls to listen to so long as you stipulate a good one and a not so good one.

- Don't choose calls randomly; use intelligent Speech Analytics Software to choose keywords, phrases used, attitudes, sentiments and acoustics.

- Allow your agent to gauge themselves against your best practice checklist, and then comment afterwards.

- Use silence, non verbal nods and lots of matching body language to encourage the reflector to talk… and we do.

- Once some actions start appearing, GROW them naturally and then wrap up with the WHY – *what* they need to do, *how* they can get there and what *you* and the business can do to support them

1 to 1 performance coaching

Theorists might prefer the 1to1 coaching with metrics and KPIs to ponder over. Some tips here:

- Let them have the metrics in advance.

- With the exception reports, focus equal time on the above average performance as opposed to the below average performance, this is a balanced performance review after all.

- Try and use a balanced scorecard approach to the metrics you measure. You could split these four ways:

  - "How well is your agent serving the customer?" – Customer satisfaction

  - "How well is your agent performing?" – Operational efficiency

  - "How well is your agent supporting sales?" – Business value

  - "How am I getting the best out of my agents?" – People management

- Always have some coaching in the metrics meetings, these are not just assessment and feedback but a chance to spot trends and determine action plans.

Group call listening sessions

Pragmatists might prefer the group interaction commenting on played-back calls, especially if you have some top performers in the group and keep it punchy. Here's some ideas:

- Choose calls carefully, some exemplars and not such good calls. Maybe choose a theme upfront.

- Sell the WIIFMs to the agents before you start. (What in it for me's)

- Keep the session to about 45 minutes.

- Ask them to complete the best practice checklists.

- Invite everyone for their opinions but keep this tight. Request one good point and one development area and ban repeating what previous agents have said.

- You don't need to chip in an opinion just for the sake of it; the art is to encourage the agents to comment on their own calls.

- My final tip is to ask the agent as to the preferred coaching, what coaching would they want from you to support their growth and how should the coaching occur. They won't give you pragmatist, theorist, reflector – that's technical jargon for you and I – but they will give you an impression to work on.

Now haven't we breathed a breath of fresh air into Peter and Alan's learning styles?

The Inside Sales Manager's Performance Cycle

Every sales led organisation has numbers. Objectives and targets. Senior sales directors are hired and fired on these so the pressure filters down to the front line sales managers to hit their targets too.

Unfortunately, this pressure continues down the line to the front line sales people.

The result?

You probably hit the numbers most of the time, but what happens when you don't, or when some of your sales people struggle?

You shout louder, you pile on the pressure, you lose people, you gain people. But performance doesn't improve, the skills and capabilities of the sales team won't advance.

Background

I first worked with the client back in 2011 when they were a fledgling firm with only a handful of salespeople. They took the plunge to expand and up-scale their operation during 2013 and 2014, and I received the call from them last week.

"Help us please Paul, we're struggling to maintain momentum, our revenue is falling, and our incoming calls are down, can you come in and help us to make calls to our existing client base to boost our revenue and help the guys hit their targets?"

"Of course I can, let me swing by later this week and we'll talk it through."

After an hour or so talking and chatting everything through, it became very clear to me that providing some training, so the salespeople could phone orphan clients, in order to generate some new business was clearly not going to work. The initial reason was that they would find the rejection of making these semi cold calls unbearable, and as soon as the phone started to ring again, they would again stop being proactive.

"How are you measuring them?" I asked. "They each have revenue targets of £7,000 per month," he responded. "Good, what are their KPIs (Key Performance Indicators)?" I continued. "That's it - £7,000 per month and we display it on a Z Graph up here on the wall".

Clearly they were being targeted and pushed around the final numbers – the revenue per month. It was on the wall and you could clearly see who was doing well and who was struggling.

I continued with my questions. "What do you talk about in your sales meetings?" "We have them each Monday, and we talk about their targets, and their performance, and what they're going to do to improve. We go around the room and ask each seller what they're going to do to hit target that week."

By the way, this is a classic error in sales management. Focusing just on the targets and the final numbers does nothing to help the salesperson to perform better. It just piles on the pressure, but many sales managers only measure this way, and harass their people to perform.

I continued. "How else do you manage your team?" "It's difficult to do much else as we don't have time, that's why we want you to deliver some training".

And at that point it was crystal clear to me what had evolved. My client had organically grown his business over the previous few years, had recruited some new salespeople, and now had a team of around 10 sellers. However, my client, who was the CEO, continued to sell to the higher net worth clients they had been dealing with for years, so had little time to do anything else apart from pursue them when they were short on targets.

Do you recognise this? Seen it all before?

In a busy marketplace, when your marketing machine is generating lots of new leads, and the phone keeps ringing, you can get away with it. But when things turn against you, for example, a quiet period, marketing failing to bring in leads, the competition raining on your parade, or a recession…you really do need to tighten up your performance sales management regimen. My client had not taken any of the actions recommended above. They had an effective marketing engine, albeit seasonal. They had a booming marketplace with an economy growing at a 3% increase in GDP year after year. They had little competition of note. Their issue was expansion. They wanted to grow their business, had recruited new sales people, and leased new office space with shiny new equipment and software.

They had grown up and matured, and I realised they needed some effective performance sales management. Allow me to explain what is needed to help them achieve their goals and stay in business, because right now, they're haemorrhaging money.

The Performance Cycle

Let's take a look at each area of the cycle and examine what the sales manager needs to do to complete the whole cycle. That's the first point to make. This growing company needs a sales manager, someone who can provide the guidance and determination to see it through. To manage a team of 12 sellers, could easily keep a full time person busy. And they do need managing; my client had neglected this because they were so busy.

Strategy and objectives

Evolve your purpose, values, culture, and overall aim of the business. Value proposition comes in here once you're clear as to what you're all about, your marketplace, and the offering you bring to the market.

Decide your route to market, how you can continue to bring in new customers, sell to these customers, and maintain a relationship with the same customers, so they come back to you when they need you again.

Engineer how and what this process looks like. We call this the sales process, it's vital to have one, and you decide how detailed it is. Be careful of falling into the trap of letting your salespeople free wheel through the sales activities. Naturally they need to bring their personality, skills, and verve into the sale, but they must follow the pattern or process that you lay out.

Next comes your KPIs. Naturally you'll have sales revenue targets, of course you will. These are known in the trade as outputs, lag indicators, or just plain and simple – the numbers. Have these, but spend more attention on other KPIs which will drive performance. Take a long look at your sales process, and decide what activities need to happen in order to achieve success and hit your targets. Prospecting calls, first meetings, written proposals, etc. You can make these KPIs and focus on the quantity of them if you wish, but better still, consider how you can measure the quality of them.

For example, appointment making calls. You can have a KPI of 10 per week if you wish. I would also want the quality to be measured, i.e. for every 3 calls, 1 appointment is made. This 3:1 ratio becomes a KPI in its own right.

These are known as activities, and lead indicators. What gets measured gets done, as the phrase goes. Strive for less focus on the targets and revenue numbers, and more focus on the myriad of activity KPIs that will bring success. So long as the activities are carried out with the pre-requisite skills, then the numbers will fall out at the other end.

It's a brave decision to focus on these and not the sales numbers, but if you do, you're well on your way to success in the cycle.

Communicate your objectives and plans

Whenever I'm asked by clients to help with re-engineering sales processes and KPIs, I always start with the concept of "ownership". The people who want to buy into all of this are members of your sales team, so ask them to create the sales process, and to determine the various KPIs they need to achieve success. The concept and the process are simple and very effective.

Communicate the objectives annually, quarterly, and monthly. Gain buy in to the objectives and finesse this by creating a motivational environment for them to operate in. Motivation is intrinsic, it comes from within. For salespeople, it's about recognition, the chance to fulfil their potential, challenging and exciting work, and constant development. It's not about reward. Reward will stimulate them, but they expect this, and more of it won't necessarily provide a motivational environment for them to excel.

Rewards are bunched up with other "hygiene" factors such as working conditions, style of management, and relations with others. You have to get these right first before you can really motivate your team to perform.

I'm going to mention training here. If any of the performance objectives are not going to be achieved due to a lack of skill or knowledge, then announce to the sellers that you have organised a programme of training throughout the year to help them achieve these objectives. This is very motivational, will allow you to ensure success, and the cost of the training can be counterbalanced by the revenue that you'll be getting when the objectives and targets are met.

Measure and monitor

My client had a giant whiteboard on the wall which measured the sales results, day by day, and also a moving annual total as a Z Graph. Granted, this is very illuminating, satisfying for the manager, and quite stressful for the sellers who saw this only as a way to drive their performance.

Your CRM system will form the foundation of any measurements, so build into this your activities based KPIs and measure them. Keep an eye on the KPIs and share these with your sellers. Put them on a whiteboard, if you want, or on your "dashboard" contained in your CRM system. These are indicators and won't tell you the whole story. Remember I mentioned that if your sellers do these KPIs and bring in the required level of skill, then they will hit their numbers. It's the required level of skill you want to monitor. And that's where coaching comes in.

Field visits are the answer where you observe, give feedback, and coach. Observe these against the sales process and create some form of observation aid which you can also use in new recruit training.

Collect forecasts from your salespeople to help measure and put together milestone objectives which measure revenue or targets over a shorter period.

Carry out regular one to ones with your salespeople to discover how they're doing, and to identify any problems, or issues that you can help with. Include feedback on their KPIs and other activities that you're measuring.

Review performance

The previous activity was essentially observing and monitoring; now we want to review performance. It's very easy to say they're not achieving target, but this is merely focusing on the output which is too late, that's why we call it a lag indicator. Performance against activities need to be reviewed here, as well as the KPIs that determine the amount or quantity and the quality of the KPIs.

Corrective action

Naturally, if performance is good or exceptional I wouldn't correct it but I would applaud it. Remember sales people thrive on recognition, so make sure you offer it. I'm going to go against the grain now and say that this praise needs to be also done in private not in public – it's just too embarrassing for the salesperson involved and just winds everyone else up. Therefore, make it private.

It's also in private that you should provide feedback on a negative performance, that's why we have performance review meetings at least monthly.

Jointly decide what you can both do to improve on performance, here's a list to remind you:

- Training in all its guises – shadowing, job rotation, workshops, reading, videos, and podcasts.

- Coaching

- Mentoring

- Counselling if the reason for the performance drop is Inner Game

- FISH to find out the cause of the performance drop.

- SPELL it out if they don't see it themselves. Particularly if the issue is attitude not skill.

- Inject something new into the motivational environment you provide.

- Bring someone else in.

The sales meeting

My final ingredient is the sales meeting. I've not mentioned it before because most are badly run. A true sales meeting should be all about helping the team to hit its numbers. The role of the sales manager, their core reason to be, is to achieve the sales objectives of the business through the team at their disposal. So the sales meeting should have activities which include training, coaching, role-playing, idea generating, and sharing best practices. It is not a place for checking sales results and asking them what they're going to do to improve.

That's just counterproductive and de-motivational.

Summary

This is my blueprint for what a successful sales manager needs to do. My client needs to do all of these things and he'll see his business results improve, and become consistent. He can then safely upscale his operation, since he now appreciates the value and true role of the sales manager.

How To Set Up a Virtual Video Studio

Chapter Summary

It's all-pervasive nowadays, and each winter brings semi lockdowns at a rapid pace; the requirement won't go away. Working from home makes virtual training even more desirable and essential each year.

But we know that, don't we?

This chapter has a straightforward aim. To encourage you to move beyond the laptop model to some kind of Studio or room where you can emulate real-world training and presenting. Even if everything you need is stored in a pilot case allowing for portability.

Or you adopt a permanent home for your studio; that's your choice. So long as you take the first step to untethering yourself from a "sitting at your laptop on the desk" scenario.

Let me explain how.

My First Foray into a Studio

My first foray into online presenting came in 2006 with a programme called DimDim. Don't get me started on that name; it's now long "gone-gone". Dimdim was acquired by Salesforce.com for $31 million in 2011. And it worked just fine.

Goto was available but terribly expensive. Both only allowed voice-over PowerPoint presentations with little or no speaker video, let alone attendees.

I realised it wasn't right even then. I dreamt of having the tech emulate or copy how we operate in a face-to-face environment one day. I kept this dream alive during the latter years and into the pandemic, knowing that this was the way forward. I wanted to emulate the face to face experience in a virtual classroom environment.

Along came Zoom, Teams et al., each capable of beaming full video of everyone involved. I could now copy real-world training rooms with rapid broadband speeds.

However, people still defaulted to laptops playing PowerPoint slides with a presenter narrating these from a small thumbnail image in the top corner. Most attendees blank their videos and mute their sound, and the whole experience was less than inspiring.

This may resonate with you. Not because you have many choices. Armed with the firm's laptop, a built-in webcam, and a dining room table, there's not much you can do to advance yourself.

The Studio is the Answer

In 2015, I began to build my first Studio, which may sound rather glamorous as it really was only a spare bedroom. In 2019 I began excavating a basement in our house and created an all-singing video studio. It measures 13 x 10 feet, smaller than most bedrooms, but it's big enough.

The Studio is the answer. Flexibility is also the solution. You may need portability, so I will show you how to fit the kit into a pilot case and wheel it around. However, a permanent structure or room housing your equipment is ideal.

You might consider a room at home, a spare room in the office or even convert an existing small meeting room into a video studio.

The Studio Emulates Real Life

Remember your aim is to emulate the real-life experience of a physical meeting room. Let's remind ourselves how this works. A trainer or speaker usually hovers around the front of the room, and attendees typically sit around a desk or a U shaped table.

At the front are the visual aids. A screen to project PowerPoint, a flipchart or a whiteboard. Some have Smart Boards, but these are just glorified touch-screen computer monitors.

The speaker can interact with the people, and she can use whatever visual stimulates and adds to the message. Everything is being used together seamlessly. She typically stands when presenting and actively engages the group in conversation around the topic.

This is your aim but to repeat online. Let me explain the kit you need to add to your purpose-built or converted room. Your space doesn't have to be significant. I operate from a 13 x 10-foot room.

Imagine a computer mouse on a mouse mat able to control a much bigger monitor, often 3 or 4 times its size. That's how it's done online.

Let's talk kit now. Which, of course, will evolve over time. However, many video kits, such as camera technology, matured a few years ago. After all, a Carl Zeiss lens is a Zeiss lens.

The Studio on a Minimum Budget

- Space to present – I have 2 metres square to physically move around in. Recall my mouse and mouse mat analogy. You're the mouse, and the space is your mouse mat.

- 2 computer screens positioned at eye level – bear in mind you'll be mainly standing or perched on a high stool. These are to see your people.

- Headset microphone – USB connected to give you the freedom to talk and hear your attendees – note no cable.

- A decent webcam on a tripod perched behind and above your monitors. See if you can buy one with autofocus and software to operate the zoom.

- A mouse clicker that moves your slides forwards and backwards.

- A whiteboard or flipchart plus pens (large ones).

- Lighting in front of you. Possibly on the ceiling or on tripods or stands.

- Broadband connected to your PC via an ethernet cable – don't rely on Wi-Fi.

The Studio on a Maximum Budget

- Blackmagic Atem Mini – video streamer.

- HDMI Cameras – DSLR – these are the ones with the lens that protrudes from the camera giving you the ability to zoom manually. Ideally, a couple of cameras provide you with a couple of fixed angles.

- Tripods to house the cameras and cables to connect the Atem Mini.

- 4 computer screens are attached to a well-powered PC (not a laptop).

- PowerPoint from a separate laptop connected to your Atem Mini gives you the ability to switch the view to your slides just by pressing one button on the Atem.

- A sound speaker system attached to your PC to hear your people.

- Lapel microphone wirelessly attached to your PC or Atem Mini.

- Whiteboard and/or flipchart – Whiteboards are preferred. Flipchart paper just doesn't look right on camera. Think of a Vienetta. Google this – they're delicious.

- A pull-down green screen allows you to appear in front of your slides in full view.

- A variety of lights on stands to light up you, the green screen and whiteboard.

The Studio as a Portable option

Shelley and I spend a lot of time in Edinburgh visiting our daughter Jess in their flat. We hire a small flat on Airbnb, which has fast Wi-Fi, and I like to run live online sessions whilst we're there.

So I have a mobile version of my Studio – not ideal, but it allows me to perform as well as possible. Particularly useful for small group events, one to one coaching and such. Here's what's in my bag:

- Laptop – obviously and hooked up to the Wi-Fi – the router is close by with no thick walls or microwave ovens in the way.

- Tripod and flat stand for the laptop, which will be at eye level.

- Ring light to perch behind the computer – this light attaches to a USB port on the laptop, so no extra power cable is needed.

- Logitech Brio Webcam with a clamp so that it hangs on the top of the laptop.

- Headset and microphone attached – USB connection to laptop.

- Extra USB gadget to allow more open ports on the laptop.

- Sticky whiteboard plastic. These look like cling film and come out of a dispenser. Take a slice and stick it to the wall. Hey, presto – one whiteboard.

- Software – I use Logitech Capture – to allow me to stream a picture in a picture for my slides and me. That way, the slides appear alongside my video image.

- Capture allows me to resize my video image perfectly and have slides to my right or left. Clever and simple.

- This all fits neatly into a pilot case, so I'm incredibly portable.

The Studio Photos

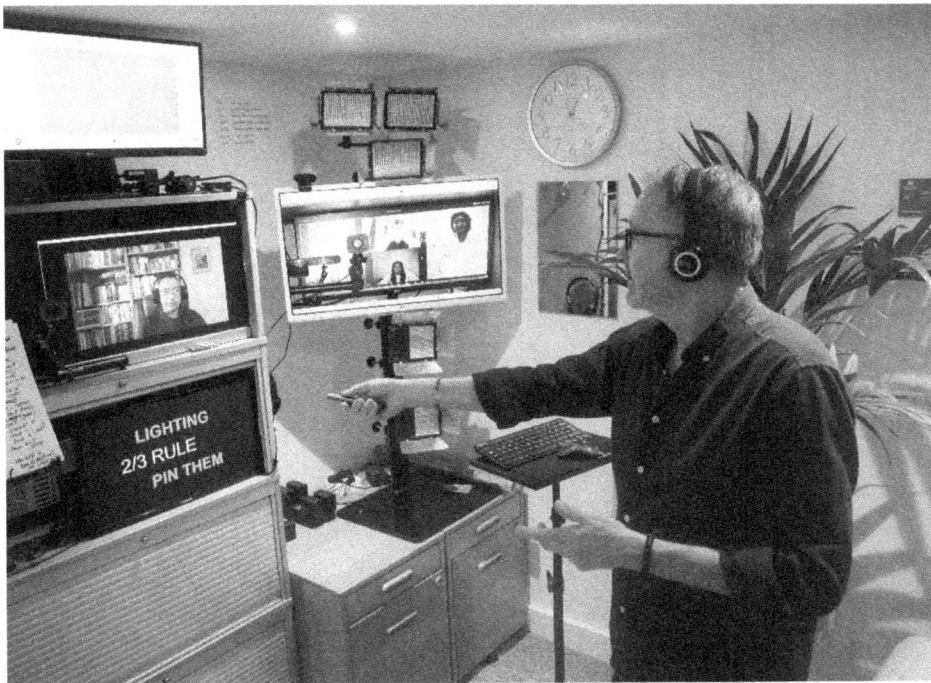

A Field Guide to Live Video Selling

Chapter Summary

This field guide was designed for you – the professional B2B or B2C salesperson – to quickly adapt to the Live Video Selling world. Inside the handbook, you'll see all of the processes, skills and techniques you need to master to achieve in this new medium, which isn't going away.

An essential Field Guide.

At the back of the guide, you'll find a convenient checklist that you can use to self-assess your progress. All Sales Managers will find this essential when observing your salespeople, which is straightforward when selling on video.

We'll be adding to the guide as technology evolves and improves rapidly over the next few years.

Adapting Your Sales Process for Live Video Selling

- Gone are the days, or at least post–lockdown, when in-person sales meetings happen, so maximise and accelerate your sales process to enable Live Video Selling.

- Shorten the meetings, and cut down the aims for each session—separate sessions for rapport and trust-building, discovery, presentations, negotiations etc.

- Meetings no longer than 20 minutes and scheduled off the hour, i.e. 10.10 or 15:25. This encourages attendance and punctuality rather than on the hour. Twenty-minute slots are more likely to be agreed or fitted around your customers' busy schedules.

- Tightly agenda every meeting.

- Schedule each meeting using Calendar Invites with Zoom/Teams invite logins and include the list.

- Bring in other team members into discussions to add variety and engagement – agenda their input strictly.

- Stretch your sales process if need be; decisions are made slower in a "down" economy.

- End each meeting with a call to action, summarise these via email using the same calendar invite entry on Office 365 and link these, Velcro fashion, to the next meeting. Always have a link for every meeting – a glue.

Creating Your Professional In-Home Studio – a Reminder

- A professional home studio doesn't always involve a dedicated room or study. However, this is preferable to ensure privacy and minimal noise and disruption from family/home life.

- At home, create a "Zoom Zone" or "Teams Terrain" where the background is conducive to a professional image. This zone, which sits behind you, should be pleasant to the eye and maximise the rule of thirds. Visualise your screen space with three vertical and three horizontal lines creating nine equal-sized boxes. Position your head and shoulder in the left or centre box with your eyes in the top bar. Place eye-pleasing items such as plants and photo frames on the other side of your space.

- The wall can be blank; it better to be so rather than gregarious wallpaper. Head over to YouTube to watch some professionally produced videos, and you'll notice this tip in action. Have your Team Terrain or Zoom Zone available to you in your home office or anywhere in the house that works. Remove any sign of a bookshelf – that's just been abused during the lockdown.

- I have a video studio for my online workshops with whiteboards and green screens, but you don't need to go to that extent.

- Line up your background before any video call, so it's perfect as soon as the call starts; there's nothing worse than adjusting your webcam as you're introducing yourself. It should be instantaneous.

- Be wary of digital backgrounds – they never look right and appear surreptitious. Have you ever bought from a website with no contact details, address or phone/email? Digital backgrounds seem to hide something. They never look good unless you have a well-lit Green Screen behind you. Be careful of the pop-up company adverts behind you as well. If you were in a client meeting in person, you wouldn't remove a pop-up banner from your briefcase and display it behind you, would you? So why do it on Live Video Selling?

- Dress well and appropriately for your meeting; you can slightly dumb down your appearance. The ties are usually only for professors appearing on the nightly news.

- Eliminate noise wherever possible. A closed-door does the job. Use Zoom's AI setup to remove unwanted noise – it's remarkably proficient at doing this.

- Rid yourself of any distractions. Cats and dogs were OK during the lockdown, quite the novelty, but that newness has now worn off.

- Too far away? Or too close. Can you fit your head and shoulders onto the screen without being too distant or in "their face?"

- Be aware of the angle of your webcam. Place the camera lens so that it's level with your eyes. Place this on some books or a purpose-built stand if you're using a laptop. If you have a moving webcam, purchase a gooseneck tripod and position the camera so that it's level with your eyes.

- Focus on your office set up in your conference room or work desk. These tips can be imitated in your in-person office, particularly any open-plan office you use. Backgrounds can be tricky, but an office scene is harmonious so long as it's neat. Sound is the big issue, and a stylish headset is a must for in-office Live Video Selling.

- If you have a conference room setup, then you probably also have a budget to kit it out professionally to enable groups of you to present and receive customers on video. Logitech does some perfect kit, so google them.

Prospecting, Lead Generation and Discovery and Presenting Tips

- Social selling can be adopted seamlessly with Live Video Selling. The use of the internet to find, research and discover potential customers and prospects is essential. Arguably, this is marketing, but modern professional salespeople adopt Personal Marketing concepts and do much of this themselves. Marketing teams are migrating into different focus areas now; professional salespeople conduct personal marketing.

- Old fashioned cold phone calling is a relic of the 1990s – some still advocate this but look at them closely, and they probably still live in the 90s or at least gained their sales spurs in that decade.

- The key is connecting seamlessly marketing with selling. Selling starts with a rapport and discovery stage with Live Video Selling doing the work.

- From the LinkedIn typed chat, encourage a meet, the first face to face contact. Do this via Video for 10 minutes, assessing joint chemistry and rapport. Phone calls can work, of course, but many of your potential customers, in the B2B space are readily available via Video Call and prefer this method. Suggest, and you will be rewarded.

- Use screen-share regularly to provide variety and visual stimulus – websites, PDFs, sales aids, video – can all be shared well.

- Collaborate with your customer if you feel it would add value. Use a shared PowerPoint or whiteboard and encourage the customer to co-operate online. For example, you could put the five main challenges other customers face and ask them to annotate with a "tick" or "cross" next to the words. Or you could use icons or pictures to add flavour. Naturally, you'll want to ensure the customer is "up for this" – some are, some aren't – and the kit they're using may or may not be conducive; for example, a touch screen may enable them to draw quickly. Collaboration builds commitment.

- Stand and deliver, sang Adam Ant in 1980. The girls loved him; your audience might adore you more if you stood and gave your presentation. Have a delivery zone where you can move around a little, autofocus your camera and put it at eye level, avoiding nostril view. Try it and see

- Use "you" more than the omnipresent slides. Many speakers like to hide behind the slide deck, relax in their chairs and talk. These webinars don't cut much nowadays; your audience wants more of you. So more you, fewer slides.

Sharpen the Saw – Skills to Develop

You want to sharpen your skills with your new kit and sales process.

- Mature your empathy capability. Understand their position and point of view. Are they at home, suffocating with lockdown, panicking over the down economy or struggling with too much business?

- Become adept at reading faces. Body language reading is for in-person meetings – the stroll from reception, the small talk in the elevator, and the chat over coffee – all allow you to assess their body language. On video, that's not possible. Focus on micro expressions, facial colour tone, learn eye movements (NLP up, down etc. – thinking styles).

- Be aware of your resting face. Do you grimace, smile, glare or look downright angry? Your customer will be looking at your face continuously and making judgements just so you learn to create a halfway house resting face. Not the put on smile that most Zoomer's put on when they see their face on the screen, but a cross between thinking and a smile.

- Listen loudly and pause more regularly. Pausing helps the other person jump in the say something, particularly useful when more than two of you are on the call. When in-person, it's the subtle cues that help us step in and talk. You don't have this on video, so pause more and allow the conversation to be two-way.

- Summarise more often when live video selling. Summaries are valuable sales tools anyway, primarily important on video as they allow the customer to digest everything, confirm you've heard them and move the conversation on. You'll be running shorter meetings on-screen so summaries can stop waffling and diversifying the conversation off track.

- Your ability to ask quality questions is even more vital when live video selling. You might get away with second-rate questioning in person because your body language and non-verbal skills encourage the customer to say more. On video, this can't be relied upon. Use open questions, of course, but learn to use Power Open Questions. These questions cause the customer to respond, "that's a good question." Think back to the last time a customer said this to you, and you probably just asked the finest question of your sales career.

- Power questions are short, open, curious, genuine and valuable. "Talk me through…" is an excellent example, "what brings you to that thought?" is another.

- Use stories to illustrate. Live video selling can be tricky to concentrate on, especially when presenting with few visual aids. Turn this into a short, engaging story, and you'll regain the customer's attention. Craft your stories – google story selling for ideas – learn and curate them for varying needs. For example, have stories ready for – comparing with competition, your crucial selling points, previous customer objections, client success stories, why they should use you rather than Acme etc.

- Refine your facilitation skills for when you bring others onto the call. For example, you may bring in the product specialist, legal people or your sales manager to help with the call's objectives. Become the orchestra's conductor; otherwise, they'll dominate or won't know when to contribute. You take control and bring people in and out of the conversation. Live video selling requires conducting.

- Ramp up your vocals and sound. Either get some software to do this or learn to sound like a TV presenter or newscaster. Smarten up your vocal cosmetics – pace, tone of voice, resonance, range, emphasis.

- Eye contact. Since lockdown, the internet has well documented this skill; however, staring at your camera lens is not the answer. No one ever won a sales contract by staring at the customer's eyes throughout the hour-long in-person meeting. It's not natural, so neither is continuously staring at the camera lens. Newscasters do this because they speak to a camera with millions of people watching. You're not. You're engaging with an individual, so adopt your in-person eye contact routine with the lens as a part of their face.

- Position your camera lens as close as you can to their eyes on the screen. You can use a gooseneck tripod to place the webcam right in front of the screen – you can give them proper eye contact and look at the lens simultaneously. Alternatively, move your gaze from their eyes on the screen to the camera lens naturally, so a few seconds on their eyes, then over to the lens for a couple of seconds, then away to the left for a second or two, back to their eyes and so on. Make it natural.

- Test closing. Without body language to read, the imaginary traffic light signal of red, amber and green is impossible. This buying signal technique works very well in person but not on-screen, so adopt verbal test closing more. "How does that sound, Jenny?" or "what are your thoughts so far?" or "Are we both on the right lines here?". You could sprinkle in a yes tag if you want, couldn't you. How's this article reading for you so far?" It's proving rather useful, isn't it" "You'd like to finish it, wouldn't you?"

- Note-taking is an art whether you're in person or on camera. Note-taking on camera can appear stilted and disingenuous towards the customer, so learn to jot down key points or mindmap. Suggest to the customer that you want to make a few notes and say when you are. More signposting of your actions is needed on camera.

Trust Building on Camera

- Trust building or maintaining a rapport can be a little trickier on camera. In-person gives you many more opportunities – talking about the game on Sunday works well, or chatting about their family outing whilst riding the elevator. Or matching and mirroring their body language and style.

- On camera, adopt a few additional measures. Use social media to collate a picture of your customer. LinkedIn can help. Googling can reveal aspects of the person.

Using Visual Aids – PowerPoint

- Using visuals is essential; PowerPoint is the go-to. Live video selling with PowerPoint requires dramatically different slides.

- Follow the 3 to 4-second rule with visuals. Every 3 to 4 seconds, there needs to be a change: an animation movement, a new slide, something different. A one-word slide followed by another to mirror your sentence works well—large imagery. Think Hollywood movies and Steven Spielberg – always exciting, continually moving. Keeps attention.

- No bullets please, we're British. Or American. Bullets are a relic of the 1990s and kill people.

- There are many more tips available to maximise your PowerPoint; invest in some online training; you'll be glad you did.

- Collaborative whiteboards replace the paper we all used to use. A real whiteboard can be helpful behind you but requires special lighting and positioning. Virtual whiteboards can be used easily with a touch screen or stylus.

- Blend your face with your visuals. Many of your customers will be using a monitor with just enough space for your visuals. Use software to blend your face and your visuals. Zoom and Teams now can do just this. Don't hide behind your visual aids and be just the voice behind the scenes. Live video selling is not running a webinar; they were invented in the 90s and should be banished to that decade along with Grunge music, Blockbuster Video and Tamagotchis.

Video Selling Checklist

Professional in-house studio adopted

☐ "Zoom Zone" or "Teams Scape" created

☐ Background synchronised before the call

☐ Digital background fit for purpose, green screen

☐ Noise eliminated

☐ Distractions minimised

☐ Webcam level with eyes

☐ Camera image using the rule of thirds

☐ Good lighting in front and above

☐ Visuals used "real" whiteboard, flipchart, hand-held board

Tech Check

☐ Internet via ethernet or Wi-Fi stable

☐ External webcam used

☐ HD image on internal cam

☐ USB mic used

☐ Headset used

☐ Large or multiple screens evident

☐ Tech Plan B is available

Competent with using Tech

- ☐ Setting up meetings
- ☐ Document sharing, programmes open with handouts etc.
- ☐ PowerPoint Screen show
- ☐ Annotation on screen for collaboration
- ☐ Pinning video
- ☐ Cloud or local recording
- ☐ Sharing video clip with sound
- ☐ Screenshots – hard copying
- ☐ Muting sound
- ☐ Gallery/speaker view toggle
- ☐ Competent use of all controls in Zoom/Teams

Online Sales Skills Checklist

- ☐ Empathy evidenced
- ☐ Trust built
- ☐ Matching customers where appropriate
- ☐ Facial language read and used
- ☐ Resting face conducive
- ☐ Signposting agenda throughout
- ☐ Listened loudly
- ☐ Paused more often
- ☐ Summarised often
- ☐ Power questions asked
- ☐ Stories/metaphors used
- ☐ Facilitation skills evidenced
- ☐ 80:20 Rule in Discovery
- ☐ Voice pace matched with customer
- ☐ The vocal range of voice used

☐   Voice volume appropriate

☐   Eye gaze maintained

☐   Visual aids used

☐   Test closing used

☐   Note-taking without distracting

☐   Stand when presenting

☐   No hiding behind slides

PowerPoint Competence

☐   Shared effortlessly

☐   Switching between full camera and slides

☐   3 to 4-second movement rule

☐   Visual stimulus

☐   SmartArt used

☐   Bullets list more graphical

☐   Collaborative digital whiteboarding

☐   Face and visuals on the same screen

No Nonsense Inside Sales

How To Present Visually Virtually

Chapter Summary

A step-by-step guide to using visuals online to enhance your virtual presentation rather than a dull, listless voice-over PowerPoint.

I've been a keen student of online presenting since my first webinar in 2006. Being constrained to sharing PowerPoint with a voice-over seemed old-fashioned to me even in 2006. I yearned to emulate real-life presenting but in the online space. But the technology wasn't available.

It is now, but very few presenters use it preferring to display a shared screen of PowerPoint visuals with a voice-over coming from a tiny face in the corner.

It can be different. And it should be. Let me show you how I've become quite adept at it. Presenting like in real life but online.

The Real-World Comparison

Let me take you back to the last in-person presentation that you enjoyed. I think you can recall a good presenter engaging with you, giving you eye contact and expressing their character. Attractive, with stories, metaphors and clear diction. Maybe some humour but particularly stimulating.

She has visuals, probably a large screen showing excellent PowerPoint. She stands to the side, maybe in front, as she moves around the "stage". She interacts with her visuals which add massive value to the topic. She is the main focus of your attention and uses visuals to back up and further enhance the message.

Not always expected in the corporate world, but I'm sure you can remember a similar real-life presentation.

The trick is to emulate this in the online environment. Let me show you how.

Why Do We Need Visuals Online?

The whole point of online presentations is to utilise the power of visuals; otherwise, you might as well just be using the phone. And there's inherently nothing wrong with the phone.

Using the online platform allows coaches and trainers to add pictorials to help the person understand what they are saying. Salespeople can use visuals with clients to describe complicated concepts. Sales managers can use them to help with their coaching and 1:1s.

The main reason for using visuals is that the world is geared that way now. We all have large TV screens on the wall, view adverts on bus stops and train stations that move. Carry phones with magnificent visual displays and are glued to the internet on our laptops and tablets, with a plethora of images.

Younger generations probably are more visual now than any generation before them, having been weaned on tablets and phones since a tender age.

Visuals are ubiquitous.

Who's the Primary Visual?

The presenter, that's who. Most platforms default to the presenter sharing a screen on PowerPoint and remaining virtually hidden whilst she narrates the slides and presents the topic.

Since this is the default for most presenters, it has become the "go-to" way of presenting. I believe this is nonsense. Presenters need to learn to present to the camera lens as though they were standing in a boardroom talking to a group of people. They should "stand and deliver". No sitting at your desk talking to a laptop.

Standing is natural when presenting; you have energy, poise and volume. Find some space in your office or room where you can talk from. Your stage, so to speak.

It's not an ample space needed – 2 metres by 2 metres is more than enough to move a little, gesture with your arms and enhance your message through body language.

Position your camera at eye level to you. A tripod, a gooseneck attachment will allow you to position a separate webcam. Or you can perch your laptop on a highchair and a few books if you have to.

On the topic of webcams, ensure you have a model that is good with autofocusing, as you will be moving backwards and forwards as you speak.

Have some lighting ahead of you, behind or above your camera. You could even light the wall or background behind you. Although this isn't essential, just light your front.

Care with what's behind you just as you would when presenting for real. Because your audience will look at whatever is there.

Finally, your microphone. The superior option is to don a lapel microphone that connects wirelessly to your computer. This gives you freedom of movement. An alternative is to have a boom microphone just under the camera. The worst option is to use the webcam mic.

Now you're dominating proceedings and controlling the presentation like a conductor in the orchestra, you can point to visuals to help you support and enhance the message.

The Default Shared Screen Option

Zoom, Teams and all platforms give you the option of sharing a computer screen or application, so your audience gets to see this on their PC screen. Tiny thumbnail mages of you and the audience appear along the boundary. Still, most of the monitor is taken up with the shared screen.

All the platforms attempt to help your video image appear more graciously alongside the shared screen. These can be clunky and difficult to control whilst in full presentation flow.

You can share anything that's on your computer. PowerPoint tends to be the bookie's favourite as we all use it when presenting in real life. PDFs, a web browser, and even a digital whiteboard can be displayed.

There are hundreds of apps you can fire up offering all sorts of visual stimuli. Zoom and Teams both give you instant access to these apps. But essentially, you're just sharing a screen with your audience, and sitting tends to be your default position as you have to operate these apps from your computer. This is why most presenters sit when presenting online. Close to their mouse.

Shame that.

Let's remember that when you present in real life, you don't have the option to operate a computer mouse. On a good day, you had a clicker in your right hand, small enough to be hidden as you gestured with your audience. We'll keep the clicker online, which you use to advance PowerPoint.

Simultaneous Streaming of You and Your Visuals

Now we're stepping things up a little. Imagine the old school presentation. Your audience would see you alongside the slides. You would orchestrate the whole scene, bringing up visuals when needed. You can emulate this online with a video streaming app.

Let me explain.

Rather than relying on your webcam to send a video stream to your webinar platform, you choose a stream created by the software. This way, you select a different video option created by the software.

The software allows you to combine your PowerPoint visuals alongside your video image. Some call this picture in picture.

There are dozens of software options to choose from, and I suggest you try a few out. Capture, Vmix, Prezi; the list goes on.

I use a Blackmagic Atem Mini Extreme to do all of this for me. This clever box of tricks controls what goes into my video stream. I have eight options. My PowerPoint visuals and four camera angles in my studio. Three spares at the moment of writing.

Imagine a BBC News studio with three or four cameras showing the newsreader from different positions. I can also combine these four options to allow picture in picture. It's pretty cool, and the ultimate coolness is the four large buttons on the console that you just press once to change the view everyone sees. No fiddling with a mouse operation whilst in full presenting flow.

The picture in picture operation shows me presenting and, alongside me, my slides. I can position my sliders next to me, above me. In fact, anywhere on my screen. However, the best feature is the green screen or chroma key feature.

Behind me, attached to the wall, is a green screen that I can pull down from the ceiling. This lets me display my visuals behind me. Weatherperson style. I can interact, point to images and words and move from left to right.

Just like I used to do with an authentic audience presenting in front, I can concentrate on my presentation and my audience behind the camera lens with the touch of four simple buttons.

Livestreaming v Zoom

The last point in this section might push you beyond the boundaries of Zoom and Teams. Once you can produce a video stream created by your software, you can livestream rather than present via Zoom. Live streaming is very different to Zoom. It's a dedicated app that streams your video anywhere, live. You can stream to YouTube, a website, Facebook. The list goes on. Livestreaming allows real HD quality from your end, and your audience can pick it up on any device. Exciting.

Other Visual Options

Remember the old school presentations? Many speakers and trainers would use a flipchart or whiteboard. There's no reason why you can't do this either. So long as you have good lighting in your room, you can position a flipchart or whiteboard to allow you to use these in front of the camera lens.

It's that easy.

My Atem Mini has a camera angle to present my whiteboard behind me. I use big whiteboard markers to allow my audience to read my drawings. I like the whiteboard. It's different, very interactive and will enable me to build a picture or story as I speak.

Just like I used to do in real-world training rooms.

Mixing it Up for the Ultimate Effect

Every successful real-life training or speaking event involved mixing it up. Never would a presenter simply sit there and talk to a group for hours on end. She would present for 5 minutes, then shows some visuals, maybe some flipchart work. She might then sit down and run a group discussion interspersed with group activities.

Presenters may run a short Q&A and facilitate brief group activities but primarily present. And that's where visuals come into their own. They allow the message to hit home, help the audience engage and enjoy the topic and ultimately take action.

Remember, it's about emulating what you did in the actual boardroom. It can be done, is being done to significant effect, and you are now expected to up your game and do the same. Gone are the days when you can "get away with a slide deck" hidden discretely behind the slides sitting at your desk with a ropey webcam and tinny sound.

You owe it to your audience.

www.ingramcontent.com/pod-product-compliance
Lightning Source LLC
Chambersburg PA
CBHW051213200326
41519CB00025B/7093